THE MIDWEST
Native Plant Primer

W9-DCV-199

THE MIDWEST
Native Plant Primer

225 Plants for an Earth-Friendly Garden

ALAN BRANHAGEN

Timber Press
Portland, Oregon

Contents

Introduction

This is a book about plants native to the heartland of North America. No place else on earth has such an extreme continental climate, yet ours is a region filled with plants of every size and in every hue. In this book, I aim to inspire readers to include native plants in their home gardens and landscapes, as well as to teach home gardeners how and where to grow these Midwest natives successfully.

Humans have manipulated the landscapes of the Midwest for millennia. Long before the first English-speaking settlers arrived, grasslands had periodically advanced eastward and northward through periods of heat and drought, the habitat they required maintained by natural and man-made fires that burned a mosaic through entire landscapes. The earliest settlers described a forest that stretched from the Appalachians to the Mississippi. Much of the forest was portrayed as open woodland, with a parklike appearance of scrub and gnarly trees interspersed with grass. The prairies were celebrated as a sea of grass so vast, it stretched to the horizon. Plants filled every niche, segregated by their adaptations to various conditions, from wet to dry, muck to sand, sun to shade, and hot to cool microclimates. We like to think of these early descriptions as depicting a pristine place, but we know that the bison, elk, and other creatures along with Native Americans and their use of fire created that landscape.

◄ Brilliant summer blooms of the prairie, including compass plant, pale purple coneflower, and rattlesnake master.

Today the seas of prairies are a vast expanse of farmland, and the forest has been fragmented into smaller tracts. Open woodlands and savannas are now dense forests. The region's great herbivores no longer roam; wildfires no longer burn. Some imported plants like bush honeysuckles and reed canary grass have usurped indigenous plants in remnant wildlands. With the forces that shaped the original landscape now gone, the remaining natural areas must be managed almost like gardens to protect their inhabitants.

Native plants are important because they sustain all life in this landscape. Many animals, mainly insects, through millennia of adaptations and evolution, are viscerally linked to a specific plant; for example, the zebra swallowtail can survive only where its host, the pawpaw, grows. We know a healthy environment for humans includes a diversity of life around us. Aldo Leopold's famous words still hold true: "To keep every cog and wheel is the first precaution of intelligent tinkering." By including native plants in our home landscapes, we are helping to save this diversity, which is especially important in the Midwest's manipulated and fragmented natural landscape.

The typical suburban landscape includes a home with foundation plantings, a lawn, and some token trees and ornamental plantings. In many cases, the shade trees are native, but most of the smaller trees, shrubs, and groundcovers, including turf, are not. And where are our native wildflowers? We can do better.

What Is a Midwest Native Plant?

In North America, a native plant is typically defined as one that grew wild in a particular or defined area prior to settlement by Europeans. And what defines our particular region, the Midwest? It's the central hardwood forest and tallgrass prairie bioregions that comprise the core of the midwestern states and a bit into Canada. Thus, Midwest native plants are those that originally grew in the hardwood forests, prairies, and associated wetlands that so beautifully interface here in the heartland of North America.

Native plants and wildflowers are not necessarily the same. A wildflower can be any plant that flourishes in a particular area on its own, including those that have naturalized from foreign shores, usually aided by humans, to reach a new region. Queen Anne's lace (*Daucus carota*), chicory (*Cichorium intybus*), and oxeye daisy (*Leucanthemum vulgare*) are examples of widespread midwestern wildflowers that are native to Europe—and so are *not* Midwest native plants.

Ranges of all plants are dynamic, not static, and that creates a challenge when drawing boundaries. Recently, Arkansas native plants have crossed the border north into Missouri, whether from human aid or dispersed by birds and other wild creatures. Botanists have documented an increasing number of site collections in Missouri of trumpet honeysuckle (*Lonicera sempervirens*), American beautyberry (*Callicarpa americana*), and cedar elm (*Ulmus crassifolia*). The changing range of plants is ongoing and happening everywhere.

Land use, climate, and soils determine the range of native plants through time. Prior to settlement of the Midwest, Native Americans and lightning set widespread fires that burned across the landscape. Settlers suppressed these fires, allowing many plants formerly limited by wildfire to spread. When rural populations peaked, farmers grazed, burned, and cut wood from woodlands, keeping them relatively open. Now such places are pretty much abandoned, creating dense forests where only shade-tolerant plants thrive.

And our climate too is changing, with the Midwest experiencing increases in average temperatures, thus allowing more southerly plants to spread northward. Northern plants, especially those that were relicts in more southern areas, are dying out.

Soil type remains relatively constant in any given place and is based on its parent material, pH, and moisture availability. Many plants are adapted to specific soil conditions and so have restricted ranges defined by those soils. Sandy, loess, or more acidic soils based on igneous bedrock harbor many range-restricted midwestern plants.

▶ Bur oak is a widespread and iconic midwestern tree.

Native plants depicted and described in this book are widely available and widely cultivated, and they will perform well in gardens across most of the Midwest. More important, they will also support the native fauna, including birds, bees, or butterflies—sometimes all three. Most Northwoods, or northern relict, species are not included, as they are often very challenging to grow outside of their cool habitats.

Why Cultivate Native Plants?

What an amazing garden was here before us, surviving on native soils, with seasonal rainfall, fertilized by creatures and by their own recycling program. Growing, flowering, and fruiting in the region's growing season, in balance with a web of life that included a nearly infinite number of soil microfauna, insects, birds, and mammals, native plants were the epitome of sustainability. Why cultivate native plants? The answer is easy. To paraphrase Dr. Seuss's Grinch, pondering the true meaning of Christmas, "They grew without irrigation, they grew without hoes, / they grew without fertilization, pesticides, or Lowe's."

Cultivating native plants where they are able to thrive and watering them only until established saves our most precious commodity—clean fresh water. Planting them in the types of soils in which they grow in the wild makes them even more sustainable. Native soils have the proper fertility; you don't have to amend them. This makes the purchase of fertilizers unnecessary and reduces polluted runoff into local streams and wetlands. All this preserves our natural resources and reduces required maintenance.

There are caveats. Many soils in our manipulated landscapes have been damaged by construction, and such compacted or otherwise compromised soils must be amended unless plants that prefer (or at least tolerate) disturbed soils are utilized. Mycorrhizal fungi are especially important

◄ The beauty of native wildflowers on the Paint Brush Prairie, Pettis County, Missouri.

because they bridge the gap between soil and root, helping plants absorb water and nutrients; if they have been lost, you may have to bring some in. Plants must be irrigated after transplanting and during periods of severe drought, but they may require extra watering in altered soils because the microfauna and other soil life are not fully present to help them obtain water.

Native plants play an integral role in the web of life. The wasps and fritillaries on the milkweed flowers collect nectar for food, but in so doing they pollinate the flowers. Pollination brings about fruits with seeds and ultimately more milkweeds, so each benefits from the other. Monarch caterpillars are adapted to eat only milkweed, as is a whole "milkweed village" (there's a T-shirt) including aphids, several species of true bugs, and a moth caterpillar with a gorgeous coat of hairs—all able to feed on no other plants. A midwestern monarch needs not only a cool, montane Oyamel fir (*Abies religiosa*) forest in Mexico in which to overwinter but also a wasp or other pollinator—as does a whole cast of other creatures. A similar scenario is true for every plant and creature we see. We need this cast of characters, too, as a lot of our food requires pollinators.

Native plants are a vital component of a healthy landscape. If you embrace native plants and their accompanying balance with the web of life, you not only attract a plethora of entertaining creatures to your landscape, you also work with them as predator and prey to help keep them all in balance. Pesky bugs rarely occur in numbers that would damage your prized plants because other predatory and beneficial insects (and other wildlife, like hungry birds) are also present. This will reduce and even eliminate the need for pesticides. Many pesticides are misapplied and cause damage to the health of our environment beyond intended usage—often killing the very beneficial creatures we need.

Native plants were the original ornamental flora of this land. They define the aesthetics of the Midwest and help differentiate it from the East Coast, the South, or the Pacific Northwest. The unique aesthetic and inexplicably linked web of life is what "spirit of place" is all about. Do you want to live in Anywhere, U.S.A., on planet Earth, or do you want

A prairie remnant overlooking farmland in Winneshiek County, Iowa.

to bloom where you're planted and be a part of the nature of your place?

The trouble is, midwestern native plants have a P.R. problem. I've known native plants and native landscapes all my life and love their special beauty, but I know it's an acquired taste. With exposure and understanding, I think native plants would be more embraced. Take time to visit the Tallgrass Prairie National Preserve, Kansas State University's Konza Prairie, or the Nature Conservancy's Tallgrass Prairie Preserve in northeastern Oklahoma. And even more important—visit and support local remnants of tallgrass prairie, savannas, glades, woodlands, wetlands, or whatever you have locally that preserves vestiges of native flora. Each serves as a reservoir of the plants most adapted to the particular conditions of your region. Although virtually all these remnants are small and can no longer support keystone species like bison and prairie chickens, they may harbor other treasures of our fauna, from insects to lizards and birds. Your local remnants are the reservoir of plants and animals that, ideally and ultimately, will colonize your own garden.

Acquiring Native Plants

Many native plants are quite difficult to grow from seed, so purchasing a plant is the only option. Most states have a state nursery that provides low-cost tree and shrub seedlings, and many local and midwestern regional nurseries sell native plants and seedlings, as well as seed. When acquiring plants, ask about provenance; make sure they are nursery-propagated or divisions from gardens—not pillaged from what's left of the wild. If a plant is inordinately cheap—especially if it is one of the more slow-to-propagate spring wildflowers—it may signal that it has been collected from the wild. Local plant societies and organizations occasionally salvage wildflowers from construction projects but always after obtaining permission from the landowner.

Many Midwest native plants do not conform to nursery mass production. They are programmed to grow roots with little top growth as an adaptation to the climate. Many upland oaks, shagbark hickory, pecan, Ohio buckeye, eastern hophornbeam, leadplant, New Jersey tea, prairie and large-flowered trilliums, and other spring wildflowers grow that way. This makes them more expensive than standard nursery items, but I guarantee they will be worth the wait and added expense in the long run. Dedicated native plant horticulturists and nursery professionals are slowly cracking the code to produce many of our more difficult native plants, including orchids.

Many other native plants are not grown in quantity because the demand for them is simply not there. Every native plant purchase you make helps the cause. I dream of a time when native bulbs are as easy to purchase as tulips and daffodils. I relish the thought of lawns filled with wild hyacinth and violet wood-sorrel rather than (or at least along with) Siberian squill and crocus. I also hope to see the day when drought-tolerant, difficult-to-transplant trees and shrubs will be as readily available as red maples and invasive Callery pears. Resist the temptation to buy cheap, easy-to-produce trees that usually are shorter lived. Many of our communities' native trees are mature and not being replaced—or if they are, the replacements are clones (mostly fruitless males). We owe it to future generations to know what the real midwestern flora was. The rebirth of our priceless native flora can begin in our own backyards.

The Midwest Spirit of Place

How does one define the spirit of the Midwest? It's the blend between the verdant forests of the Appalachians on the east and the dry, short grasses of the Great Plains on the west. It lies below the cold boreal evergreen northern woods and above the great steamy southern swamps and pinelands. It is a land defined by a prevalence of open woodlands, savannas, and tallgrass prairie.

The Midwest encompasses the core of the Great Lakes and the amazingly rich soils of the glaciated Corn Belt Plains that sweep from central Ohio westward to the Central and Northern Great Plains. Here lies one of the world's richest swaths of soils—nearly half of the prime farmland in the United States is in Iowa and Illinois—drained by five of the continent's greatest rivers: Mississippi, Missouri, and Ohio to the south, Red to the north, and Saint Lawrence to the east.

◀ A premier, old-growth beech-maple forest can be seen at Warren Woods State Park, Berrien County, Michigan.

It's a landscape that is relatively flat, repeatedly scoured by glaciers in the past. The glaciers left a landscape of "prairie potholes" rich with waterfowl in the Northern Glaciated Plains, marvelous moraines in the Southeast Wisconsin Drift Plains, and remnant bogs in the southern Michigan–northern Indiana Drift Plains. Only the Flint Hills, Osage Plains, and Ozark Highlands in the west, Interior and Allegheny Plateaus in the east, and, like an island, the Driftless Area escaped. There are no mountains, except for ancient mini-remnants in the Baraboo Range in Wisconsin and the St. Francois Mountains in Missouri; even the Ozarks are flat on top. Marvelous rivers have cut into this flatness; the coulees of the Driftless Area and bluffs along the major rivers also testify to this. Great dunes of loess, the Loess Hills, flank the eastern valley of the Missouri; great dunes of sand rim the eastern and southern shore of Lake Michigan.

Subregions

From a gardener's perspective, the Midwest can be divided into three subregions: the warmer Lower Midwest, the milder Upper Midwest, and the moister Eastern Midwest.

The Upper Midwest contains some elements and remnants of the Northwoods. Some Lower Midwest trees and shrubs are not hardy in this subregion. Snow cover is reliable almost every winter.

The Lower Midwest actually has a high temperature above freezing on most days all through winter. Snow cover is not reliable and rarely lasts for more than a week. Summer heat is more steadfast, so some Upper Midwest plants can't tolerate that aspect.

The Eastern Midwest lies east of Lake Michigan and has more reliable rainfall and higher humidity. It includes the lake-effect snow lands where blankets of clouds and snow snuggle plants through the coldest winter nights.

◄ **An early summer morning in the Kansas Tallgrass Prairie Preserve.**

Today's Midwest is organized around major cities radiating out to farms wherever the soil suits cultivation. The wettest floodplains of the rivers remain intact, and areas too steep or of poorer soils still conserve relics of the native flora in both woodlands and rare prairie and savanna remnants. The tallgrass prairie and its accompanying wetlands are probably the rarest of originally widespread habitats on earth. Most exist only as tiny islands of what once was, now adrift in a vast sea of farmland.

Habitats

The actual interface between the eastern deciduous forest and tallgrass prairie, where scattered trees, shrub thickets, and woodland plants grow among prairie flora, is called *savanna*. Trees cover only 10–30 percent of the savanna, and this habitat has become extremely rare, as trees either have reclaimed such areas, making them woodlands, or have been destroyed by agriculture and development.

The term *woodland* refers to a more open forest with 30–80 percent tree cover, while *true forest* has dense tree cover over 80 percent. Even once-widespread woodlands have become solid forests now with lack of fire, grazing, and wood harvest. *Grassland* is the treeless province usually dominated by grasses and termed *prairie* in North America.

GRASSLANDS

The Midwest's grassland province is easy to define as the tall-grass prairie component: bookended on the west by the Flint Hills of Kansas and on the east by remnant prairies of Adams County, Ohio, on the edge of the Appalachian Highlands. These are the prairies of the eastern part of the continent, where sufficient rainfall allowed tall grasses to dominate. Three of the main tall grasses—big bluestem, Indiangrass, and switchgrass—are recommended in the pages to come.

▶ Oak savanna.

▲ Rough blazingstar and stiff goldenrod light up a prairie remnant in western Wisconsin.

◀ Loess Hills, Star School Hill Prairie Conservation Area, Missouri.

The drier short-grass prairie region of the Great Plains is not included here; it's a very different gardening region, with a climate and soils that won't support plants from much of the core of the Midwest.

Grasses were a major component of the tallgrass prairie, yet a simply spectacular accompanying suite of wildflowers bloomed in sequence from spring through fall between the grasses. If you have not witnessed these floral displays, get out there and immerse yourself in them.

The tallgrass prairie can be divided into many diverse habitats, but I'll keep it relatively simple here based on whether the prairie is dry, moist or medium (mesic), or wet. Dry prairies occur on thin, gravelly or sandy soils or on steep slopes that face hot, south and west afternoon sun and summer winds. Where bedrock is at the surface, these areas could be called *glades*, but there are also specific loess, sand, and gravel prairie communities and even hill or "goat" prairies—so named because they are so steep as to be grazed only by goats, though cattle still graze many of these remnants. Many shorter grasses like little bluestem and sideoats grama thrive in these types of prairie, and special wildflowers are able to survive in the harsher environment.

Mesic prairie is rare. It's what made the prime farmland of the Midwest and nearly all has been plowed for cultivation. Tiny remnants survive, many as early cemeteries and along railroad right-of-ways. The phenomenally deep and rich soils produce tall grasses and robust broad-leaved wildflowers that once were ubiquitous. Were it not for the great fires that swept across the landscape, these mesic prairies would have been woodland, so today constant management to remove woody native shrubs and trees from these tiny remnants is critical for their conservation. The magnificent mesic prairie soil will grow almost any tree.

Wet prairies had extensive stands of wetland native grasses that spread by underground rhizomes. Here, too, were many plants in the sedge and rush family. Sedge meadows are areas dominated by sedges, mainly the very garden-worthy tussock sedge.

Gensburg-Markham Prairie, ablaze with wildflowers, is a classic remnant mesic prairie in the Chicago metropolitan area.

Wet prairie/sedge meadow wildflowers, including Culver's root and Virginia mountain-mint, at Kieselburg Forest Preserve, Winnebago County, Illinois.

The mesic maple-basswood woods at Seed Savers' Heritage Farm shows a carpet of prevernal flora in Winneshiek County, Iowa.

FORESTS

The Midwest's untouched and underappreciated forests and woodlands boast some of the best and most extensive displays of spring wildflowers in North America. Midwestern woodlands are mainly found on calcareous (limestone-based) soils with a lower pH than many of the surrounding regions. These soils, rich in calcium and magnesium, support a ground flora like almost no other, much of it made up of spring ephemerals that bloom early before the trees leaf out, capturing enough sun to set seed, and wither away before trees cast midsummer's dense shade.

The Upper and Western Midwest's maple-basswood woodlands are rich soils that hold moisture. The dominant trees in this habitat are sugar maple and basswood; northern red oak and bitternut hickory are also prevalent. Many woodland spring ephemeral plants thrive in this habitat and show their best here. Any plant liking moist woodlands will do well. The soils are well drained, not too wet, and only very rarely dry in this "medium" moist (mesic) habitat.

The oak-hickory forest covers well-drained soils that dry out more often in the summer. The oak component of this forest refers to various species but almost universally includes bur oak, white oak, and northern red oak. The hickory component is shagbark hickory (and other hickories in the Lower Midwest). Oak-hickory forest can be found on warmer south- and west-facing slopes in otherwise more mesic areas. The deep coarse root systems of oaks and hickories and their open canopies allow for a more diverse ground and understory flora than other woodland types.

Beech-maple forest is confined to the Eastern Midwest—east of a line drawn north-to-south through Lake Michigan but including areas hugging the western shore of the lake in Wisconsin. Maple again refers to sugar maple, and the beech is American beech (*Fagus grandifolia*), with tulip tree and northern red oak common companions. These trees thrive on well-drained soils that stay moist year-round. Spring ephemeral wildflowers and ferns thrive here; other plants must have a high tolerance for shade.

The Upper Mississippi River National Wildlife and Fish Refuge protects extensive stands of elm-ash-cottonwood forest. View from Mt. Hosmer, Lansing, Iowa.

Wetlands known as "prairie potholes" are common in the Northern Glaciated Plains, as seen here at Ordway Prairie, McPherson County, South Dakota.

Elm-ash-cottonwood forest occurs on the seasonally wet floodplains throughout the Midwest. Its trees grow in soils that may be seasonally inundated by floodwaters, usually during the dormant season in early spring following snowmelt.

WETLANDS

Wetlands, besides the floodplain forests, were widespread across the Midwest, but many of them have been drained for agriculture. Swamps are forested wetland where water stands much of the year; they are mainly confined to floodplains and low lands surrounding lakes. Marshes are nonforested wetlands where water also stands most of the year. Fens are peaty wetlands fed by mildly acidic to alkaline groundwater; they are actually quite widespread across the Midwest. Bogs are acidic wetlands of sphagnum moss, which are raised above the influence of groundwater (receiving water only from rain); they are relicts of the retreating glaciers but a common component of the Northwoods. All these wetland habitats contribute plants to our water gardens.

SUCCESSIONAL LANDS

Many lands are successional in nature: in transition from clearing or farming and made up of plants that readily invade disturbed areas and set the stage for the habitat to change as it becomes more shaded and mature, so that other plants can thrive. Most of the Midwest's classic small trees

Lincoln Memorial Garden in Springfield, Illinois, was designed by Jens Jensen and displays the Midwest's classic small trees and shrubs.

and shrubs thrive only in these "edge" habitats between the forest and the prairie. Hawthorns, wild plums, wild crabapples, and gray and roughleaf dogwoods are prime examples.

Shingle oak is the classic oak for successional lands in much of the Lower Midwest, along with other garden-worthy native trees like persimmon, honeylocust, hackberry, and eastern red cedar—our only widespread native evergreen. In the Upper Midwest, northern pin oak takes the place of shingle oak; quaking aspen and paper birch are signature species, along with eastern red cedar. In the Eastern and Lower Midwest, sassafras and persimmon readily form thickets to heal open ground.

Learn what bioregion of the Midwest you live in and what your soils are. List the native plants adapted to your conditions as a palette from which to choose. These will be successful for you, contribute to a sustainable design, and celebrate the spirit of your place.

Selecting Native Plants

The first thing to think about when selecting plants is whether they can thrive in your garden's growing conditions. Elements to consider include your local hardiness and heat zone, your specific soils, and whether you have sun, shade, or combinations thereof. Most Midwest homeowners know a palm tree won't grow here and understand how winter hardiness is important in selecting plants, but making sure plants will grow under your particular soil and light conditions is just as important.

Once you know the soil, light, and moisture conditions of your landscape, you can move on to part two of selecting plants: picking plants that will perform a particular role in the garden. This is where you need to think about how each plant functions in the landscape.

The third consideration is often our starting point, as we usually pick plants because we like the way they look and how they make us feel. It's all about aesthetics, the art and beauty of a plant. This is the most fun and artistic part of the plant selection process. I place it last because we must not forget that the plants we choose for beauty must be able to grow and thrive where we

◀ The Missouri Botanical Garden's Whitmire Wildflower Garden at Shaw Nature Reserve is an ideal place to learn how to select native plants for a landscape.

plant them, and they must fulfill the functions we need to create a working landscape. A hodgepodge of plants selected solely for beauty and unable to survive a growing season or winter will not create a successful landscape. Aesthetics are but the icing on the cake of good planting design.

Right Plant, Right Place

Native plant promoters have spread the word that native plants are easy to grow and adapted to their homeland. For many species, this is true only if they are cultivated in conditions that mimic those where they grow in nature. Each species has a specific set of habitats where it thrives. Under those conditions, yes, native plants grow well and require little or no input like extra watering, fertilizer, and pesticides.

WATER

A site's ability to meet the water needs of a plant is critical and the place to begin when selecting plants. Most wetland (water-loving) plants will thrive in wet conditions and will grow in good soil that is not wet, but they will simply struggle in a dry site. In the same way, a plant adapted to dry conditions languishes and rots if it is too wet. There are always a few exceptions to this rule; for example, most floodplain trees are very tolerant of droughty sites, but this is rarely the case for the herbaceous plants beneath them.

SOIL

Soils dictate the availability of moisture and nutrients, so growing natives in the same soil type they "choose" in the wild is also paramount. Clay soils are poorly drained and hold moisture, becoming wet in times of heavy rain; but, because of their small particle size, they retain moisture in a drought. Sandy soils are just the opposite: their large particle size does not hold moisture, and any excess moisture drains quickly away. Silty soils have medium "just right" soil size, holding moisture so that the soil is neither too wet nor too dry. A loamy soil is the ideal three-way blend of clay, sand, and silt soil particles.

The best soil for plants contains organic matter or humus, observable as the dark color in soils. The black soils of Iowa and Illinois are the remains of thousands of years of prairie plants (and animals), especially the plants' extensive and deep roots. Organic matter holds moisture and nutrients, helps aerate soil, and provides food for a wealth of soil microorganisms. Many wetland soils have very high organic matter because the remains of plants decompose slowly when continually wet. Without organic matter in our soil, the Earth's surface would simply look like Mars.

Peat and muck are organic soils formed under continually saturated conditions. Such soils can be found in marshes, sedge meadows, and fens, where groundwater flows through bedrock and/or mineral soil. The groundwater rises to the surface, and this high water table keeps decomposing plant material saturated, which allows for the accumulation of organic soils. Most peat as a soil amendment is actually mined from acidic fens (not bogs) of the Northwoods. A true bog is raised above contact with groundwater and stays wet due to rainfall and the ability of sphagnum moss to hold water. Bogs occur, rarely, southward into the Upper Midwest. The organic soils of fens can be acid to alkaline, but commercially mined peat is acidic. Fens, though uncommon, can be found throughout the Midwest.

The pH of a soil, which changes the availability of nutrients, also plays an important role. Many plants require acidic soils (low pH) to grow well and will become chlorotic (yellowish instead of green) when grown in soils that are too basic or alkaline (high pH). Other plants prefer more alkaline soils. Across the Midwest, acidic soils are more apt to be found in areas of higher rainfall and in areas with bedrock substrate that is sandstone, metamorphic rock (like chert), or igneous rock (like granite). Limestone, on the other hand, is basic; it is found under much of the Midwest and contributes to our region's usually higher pH soils. Concrete also contains lime, which contributes to higher pH soils in many urban areas.

LIGHT

Exposure to sunlight is critical to growing a successful plant. Some plants are adapted to full sun, others to varying degrees of shade, and still others are designed to thrive in full shade and will literally burn in sun. Plants requiring full sun will be weak and languish in shade.

It's important for gardeners to know that morning sun is cooler than afternoon sun and less harsh to sun-sensitive plants, whereas the late afternoon sun is the hottest and harshest in much of the Midwest. This principle explains why a sun-demanding plant may do just fine with morning shade, as the midday and afternoon sun will make up for it. Likewise, a shade-demanding plant may do fine with morning sun, but afternoon sun would fry it.

Full sun is also harsher the farther south or west you go. A plant that thrives in full sun in the Upper Midwest may not be able to do so in the Lower Midwest, and likewise one doing fine in full sun in the Eastern Midwest may do better in some shade farther west, where conditions are more dry.

COLD AND HEAT

Hardiness, which usually refers to a plant's tolerance of winter's cold temperatures, also plays an important role. The Ohio and Lower Mississippi River valleys and Ozarks are our mildest regions; the coldest regions (USDA zone 4) are the northern and western edges of the Midwest. The Great Lakes act as hot water bottles, creating milder winter microclimates, especially on their leeward south and east sides, where lake-effect cloud cover moderates what would otherwise be colder, clear nights.

Summertime heat is another consideration for a plant's hardiness. Summer heat stresses plants, especially cool-season grasses and plants of northern affinity. Summer heat is at its worst in the southern and western areas of the Midwest and decreases the more northeastward you go. The Great Lakes tend to moderate the effects of summer heat, creating a plant-benevolent climate in much of Michigan.

Summer heat is important for growth and hardening off (a plant's preparation for winter), and most of our natives, from redbuds to hackberry, require the warm summers of the Midwest. I follow the American Horticultural Society's Plant Heat Zone Map (ahs.org/gardening-resources/gardening-maps/heat-zone-map) when describing a plant's heat tolerance or heat requirements.

———

In summary, a native plant, in the proper soils and with appropriate moisture and sunlight, is more likely to be healthy and most able to survive extremes of heat and cold. This "right plant, right place" idea also translates into pest and disease resistance and tolerance to drought. Happily, most Midwest native plants are tolerant of average garden conditions region-wide.

At Your Service

The first function of plants in the landscape is to cover the ground and prevent erosion. Most landscapes utilize turf and/or lawn grasses for this role, but many low groundcover plants are available, and actually all plants accomplish this by covering bare soil. For covering ground, you want a plant that spreads and reduces maintenance; often you want to be able to walk or play on this plant, so the plants needs to be tough as well as low-growing.

The second role of plants in a landscape is to screen. This works both ways—for example, screening includes both windbreaks that lessen the impact of cold northwestern winds and tall hedges that block unsightly views or parcel the garden into separate "rooms." For screening, we often want evergreen plants that function through all seasons and aren't open or bare in the winter. Plants that are deciduous but densely twiggy also work, or maybe you are fine with the screen simply being a baffle, especially in winter when you may not be outdoors as much.

The third main function of plants in a landscape is to provide shade. Large shade trees are a very sound investment, especially when sited so that they will cool your home

Regional botanical gardens, such as Powell Gardens in Johnson County, Missouri, are a great place to see how native plants function in the landscape.

or outdoor seating space in summer. The size of a shade plant you choose will vary, depending on your need. If you want to shade the front stoop of your house, a large shrub or small tree will do, but to shade an entire house requires a large tree.

The environmental movement has brought to light another important function of plants: ecosystem services. What's that? It's what a plant can do in the landscape to provide green infrastructure—how a live plant can provide services that were once accomplished by engineering. Examples include green roofs to deter heat gain on or from buildings; rain gardens to alleviate stormwater runoff and improve groundwater recharge; and stream or waterway stabilization through using appropriate plants rather than concrete, stone gabions, and other such man-made structures.

Green structure also includes the neglected roles plants play as host, food, and nectar to the web of life, which includes us—directly so with human-edible plants. Plants are the beginning of the food chain, but insects that evolved to feed on them are the next link that supports so much of the life around us. With population crashes of honeybees and monarchs, for example, we're reminded how important these creatures are to us—whether for the pollination of our fruits and vegetables or simply for our sense of wonder. Native plants, as the original underpinning upon which this whole web depended, play the most important role here, bar none.

Insectaries gardens are composed of plants purposefully grown to attract appropriate insects into landscapes, gardens, or farms—or to divert the ones that are not wanted. Besides attracting pollinators for pollination services, plants selected for an insectaries garden may also attract beneficial predatory insects to help control pests, or lure those pests away from other plants you wish to protect. Insectaries gardens are the mainstay of an organic garden: they work with, not against, Mother Nature.

GARDENING FOR BIRDS

Many homeowners love having birds around, considering their song and presence a vital and enlivening component of a garden. But what does it take to really have a bird-rich landscape? Water (birdbath—check), cover (your native screening hedge will do), and above all, food.

Yes, bird food comes in a bag, but watch any songbird's nest and look at what the parents are bringing their young. It's almost exclusively protein-rich invertebrates, especially spiders, and caterpillars of butterflies and, in particular, our underappreciated and abundant moths. Marketers tout plants with berries for the birds, but plants that host the most caterpillars are the best choices for a bird-rich garden. Doug Tallamy (2007) has spread this word well; his website, bringingnaturehome.net, provides a list of plants and the number of butterflies and moths they host, which is a good place to start. Native trees excel in this category, and now we know why there are no chickadees in the urban deserts of Norway maple (*Acer platanoides*), London plane (*Platanus* ×*acerifolia*), and other trees that host nary a single caterpillar for young birds to eat.

The fruits of plants, their berries and seeds, are utilized after nesting season, for sustenance. Acorns are at the top of the list, along with native cherries, dogwood berries, eastern red cedar's berrylike cones, and the seeds in pinecones and birch fruits. Provide a diversity of plants with fruit that

Grapes are a host for the pandorus sphinx caterpillar, which in turn provides protein-rich food for young birds.

Whooping cranes, seen here at the International Crane Foundation in Sauk County, Wisconsin, once nested in wetlands across the Upper Midwest.

A wild cherry sphinx moth's caterpillar feeds only on wild cherries and plums.

ripens through the season, from early summer through fall, along with those that persist into winter, and your garden will be the most bird-friendly place on the block.

GARDENING FOR BUTTERFLIES

Where do butterflies go in winter? It's surprising how few gardeners think about that, but it's the cornerstone of sound gardening for these beautiful creatures.

Each butterfly has a particular way of surviving winter, beginning with several that overwinter as adult butterflies. Yes, even in the frigid north, several species survive sheltered in cracks and crevices of wood and in outbuildings—but probably not in your butterfly house purchased for garden décor. Many survive the winter as a chrysalis hanging from a stalk, branch, fence, or just about any obscure support or, as with the skippers, as a pupa snuggled in a nest of dead vegetation. Others survive the winter as a caterpillar: a couple create little sleeping bags of remnant leaves, tethered to the plant with their silk; most simply overwinter in fallen leaves. Finally, some butterflies (hairstreaks in particular) overwinter as eggs, poised to emerge and feed on young growth. Surprisingly, almost a third of midwestern butterfly species are colonists and migrants and do not survive the winter here.

All this means that a certain level of garden maintenance is crucial to a butterfly-friendly landscape. Rake up all the leaves, cart off all the dead stems, clean up every brush pile, and you will inadvertently kill a lot of butterflies. It also highlights that all three stages of a butterfly's metamorphosis are needed and should be accommodated. You may apply pesticides thinking you are not hitting a butterfly, but are you impacting its unseen eggs, caterpillar, or chrysalis?

Most butterflies need a specific set of related host plants for their caterpillars to eat and grow and make more butterflies. Provide the host plants, and the butterflies will find you and colonize. Adult butterflies need nectar or other sustenance to survive, so planting nectar-rich flowers or putting up a butterfly feeder, filled with spoiled fruit, does the trick. If you plant and maintain properly, butterflies will come and certainly enrich your backyard gardening experience.

Moths are even more important to a healthy garden's web of life, but they don't get the respect they deserve. They require the same gardening plant selection, care, and maintenance considerations as butterflies, as they too have a complete metamorphosis, from egg to adult.

Aesthetics

A beautiful plant is often referred to as an ornamental, and certainly every plant in this book has appealing characteristics that contribute to its ornamental effect. These attributes can arise from the overall form or shape of a plant, its foliage, bark, and stems, or (most often) its flowers and fruit. In the end, we must choose and combine beautiful plants aesthetically—taking into consideration their seasonal colors, textures, tastes, and fragrances—for a well-designed landscape.

FORM

Plant forms range from prostrate (hugging the ground) to vase-shaped (growing upward yet spreading and weeping outward toward the top). For woody plants that don't die back in winter, form is a year-round attribute that is present in the landscape in all seasons. Use plants with striking forms as focal specimens.

FOLIAGE

Except for evergreens, the foliage of a plant is an ornamental attribute confined to the growing season. Some plants have bluish or silvery leaf surfaces because of waxy coatings or silky hairs present to help control a plant's water loss or as protection against harsh sun. Often this characteristic is just on one side of the leaf, creating an interesting bicolored effect. Swamp white oak is a great example: the upper side of the leaf is the usual green whereas the underside is whitish; this characteristic can be seen from afar as the breeze blows the leaves to show their undersides.

You can actually create quite a striking landscape simply by harmonizing and contrasting the leaf textures of

Beautiful fall color and impressive form make sugar maple one of the most beloved Midwest native trees.

The heart-shaped leaf of eastern redbud adds interest to the landscape.

plants. Plants with smaller leaves are considered to have fine texture; plants with large leaves are considered coarse. Leaf sizes also affect how we perceive a landscape. Plants with tinier, fine-textured leaves actually make an object look bigger because of the added detail, but large-leaved plants do the opposite and can be used to make an overwhelming space or object appear smaller. The most delightful spaces utilize a full range of leaf textures.

The fall color of deciduous plants is a major attribute to consider when you are selecting native plants for your garden. The shape of leaves also can be ornamental, as unusual outlines attract attention; sassafras with its various mitten-shaped leaves, tulip tree with its tulip flower–shaped leaves, or redbud with its heart-shaped leaves can be sited to take advantage of these shapes. Plants with finely divided or intricately lobed leaves or with small leaflets can display the same fine-textured quality as those with small leaves.

BARK AND STEMS

Characteristics of bark and stems of plants, including color and texture and even scent, are aesthetically pleasing and can be highly ornamental. Paper birch, with its striking white exfoliating bark, is what first comes to mind when midwesterners think about ornamental bark. Bark varies from smooth and light to ruggedly furrowed and near black. Some shrubs (red-osier dogwood, for example) have red or otherwise colorful stems.

FLOWERS

Flowers are the favorite ornamental attribute of plants and the foremost reason plants leave the garden center destined for your home landscape. Whether its colorful spring bloom on small trees and shrubs or the continuing bright wave of herbaceous perennials and summer annuals, the challenge is to select and orchestrate a sequence of blooms on various plants through the growing season, from spring through fall. Such a landscape provides beauty for the entire growing season.

FRUIT

The greatest ornamental character of many plants is their fruit. The best fruiting season for most plants is fall and even on into winter, when the fruits really stand out; for example, the brilliant red berries on American highbush-cranberry are showiest in a snowy landscape, colorfast through the worst arctic blast. Herbaceous plants are too often ignored for their fruit, but this is one of the finest attributes to consider for the winter garden. Many of our midwestern native plants have tasty fruits from berries to nuts; less familiar are those with delicious tubers, stems, or flowers (or nectar-rich flowers highly desired for honey). Even when all the mulberries, blackberries, and strawberries are gone, we can taste pawpaws in September, persimmons after frost, and American hazelnuts later in autumn. Who said a landscape can't be tasty as well as beautiful?

COLOR

Our most important sense in the garden is sight, and no part of this is more enjoyable than experiencing color. Blue may be the most widely loved color, but we all have personal favorites. And don't discount how color in a landscape

The colorful berrylike cones of eastern red cedar are used in flavoring.

makes you feel. We often overlook that aspect of color, but by making thoughtful plant selections, you can really improve your well-being and enjoyment of a landscape. If you want to sit and relax after a hard day's work, choose cooler colors—green, blue, and lavender—along with white and off-whites, including pale yellow and pink. The white and whitened color show up well in evening light, too. Want an outdoor seating area that energizes you? Select vibrant reds, oranges, and golden yellows, or vivid purples. How about a winter's day—you look outside, and what do you want to see? The warm colors of fruits, berries, and twigs really stand out in the drabber season.

FRAGRANCE

Nothing evokes memories more strongly than scent. I can't imagine spring without the scent of wild plums blooming—bringing back memories of my grandparents and their farm. All too often we don't even bother to smell the flowers anymore, and this is a sad state of affairs when it comes to native plants. What does a swamp milkweed smell like? How about a Maximilian sunflower? If you don't know, you are missing something special. Add that to your bucket list of things to embrace next time you see them.

Consider siting fragrant plants near a front door, but especially around an outdoor deck or patio where people spend time outdoors. Most plant scents are based on their flowers, but some plant fragrances come from foliage. The scent of eastern white pine is one of the first that comes to mind, but I cannot help sampling many native mints by rubbing or picking a sprig of their leaves. Other favorite scents are emitted by scraping a twig or snapping dead twigs, including lemony sassafras, colognelike spicebush, and oil of wintergreen from yellow birch. Never underestimate the role plant fragrances can play in a successful garden, and be sure to include several to add to your everyday experiences in the home landscape.

Designing with Native Plants

What comes to mind at the mention of the terms *Japanese garden*, *English garden*, or *tropicalismo garden*? We have pretty good ideas of design principles for those styles, but what makes a midwestern garden? It's one that reflects our native landscape and native plants. Prairie-style architects like Frank Lloyd Wright and E. Fay Jones and landscape architects like Jens Jensen, O. C. Simonds, and Alfred Caldwell probably best captured what would be called a midwestern style. Most homeowners and gardeners, on the other hand, think in terms of the style set by real estate standards of curb appeal, which has led to homogeneous designs that create order but do not reflect the inherent beauty of individual places. We can fix that, simply by utilizing more of our Midwest native plants.

◄ Native wildflowers mix seamlessly in a border at Powell Gardens, Missouri.

First Things First

The design process described here will ensure that you select plants workable for your site without added inputs—which means that whatever your garden style, you will be gardening sustainably. When the right plant is put in the right place, its need for fertilizer, watering, and pesticides is greatly reduced. A happy plant is more vigorous and resistant to weather calamities and pests.

INVENTORY

To create a successful planting design that utilizes native plants to their optimum, you must begin by doing an inventory of your planned garden's site. Foremost is to identify the soils on the site. Are they wet, moist, or dry? Composed of sand, loam, clay, or gravel? Is there bedrock and, if so, what kind of stone is it? It's ridiculous to amend a site for your desired plants. Instead, pick plants that will thrive under the existing soil conditions. When in doubt, check your local soil survey and/or get a soil test.

Next, know your site's orientation. Here in the Midwest, it is critical to know north from south, east from west, because of the angle of the sun and where it casts cooler shadows, where it beats down most intensely (from the southwest), and how the sun changes through the seasons. The sun rises directly in the east on the vernal and autumnal equinoxes, but rises in the northeast in summer, southeast in winter.

The midwestern winds are also a factor, almost universally southwesterly in summer and from the northwest in winter. You even have to think about the aspect of the land. Is it flat? Is it sloping, and if so which direction? Note these variations if you have topography. Those who garden on the east sides of bluffs never see the sunset and have a much more sheltered site; those on the west sides of a hill may never see the sunrise and may get baked by the afternoon sun.

The inventory should note all existing plants. This is a great clue in interpreting the site's conditions and an indicator of what plants will do well in there. Gardeners with a bare, blank slate can look nearby for such plant clues. Trees are your best indicator because they have been there a long time.

A good inventory must also map all utilities, including overhead and underground wires, gas lines, water and sewer lines, and septic fields, so that plantings are compatible with and allow access to such infrastructure, thus preventing future headaches. You also want to call 811 and get underground utilities flagged, a service provided in all regions to prevent homeowners and contractors from accidentally digging into them.

ANALYSIS

Once you've identified existing plants on or near your site, look into the conditions under which they thrive. What are you doing with that research? You are analyzing the situation. Do the same for the soils: analyze the conditions and note any anomalies. It is often best not to fix them but to work with them. Don't forget compass directions and the sun and wind changes through each season. Think of where sunny and shady sites are, how to screen the southwestern sun from your home or outdoor seating space in summer. Note to block the cold northwesterly winds in winter.

Here's an example based on my own experience of buying a home. Since it's in a rural setting, I looked at the county's soil survey and learned that I had a uniform droughty clay soil, shallow to limestone bedrock in places. I inventoried where there were exposed rocks. The ridge-top property sloped eastward, draining into a ravine to the southeast. I noted the directions and existing large trees to the southwest that cool the house in afternoon; to the northwest, shingle oaks with marcescent (held through winter) leaves made a nice windbreak. The north and east sides of the house reflected a more cool and moist microclimate, the west side of the house was hotter and drier.

The existing trees were all second-growth species (shingle oak, honeylocust, black cherry, elms, hackberry) that are known to be very drought tolerant. Under the trees grew roundleaf groundsel, so I knew I would be able to grow woodland wildflowers that thrived in dry upland woods. An open meadow area to the south had milkweeds and a few other prairie plants—indicators of well-drained, dry soils. That demonstrated that upland, dry prairie species would do well in that site. No trees or wildflowers indicated moist or wet conditions.

The location of the site southeast of Kansas City places me in the Osage Plains ecoregion, where plants from the Lower Midwest will thrive in winter hardiness zone 6 (USDA) and summer heat zone 7 (AHS). My droughty upland soils indicated that I should choose from a palette of plants from the oak-hickory forest and dry prairies to fit the horticultural restrictions of the site without extra water or soil amendments.

SCHEME

Putting together a basic scheme is the final step in the design process. Everyone wants a beautiful garden that is easily cared for and a sound investment. But since you're reading this particular book, you're probably also interested in a landscape that celebrates spirit of place; a garden that is ecologically balanced and sustainable; a yard that includes edible and medicinal plants; plantings that attract birds and other wildlife; insect-friendly borders that support bees, pollinators, butterflies, moths—and so on.

So what is your style? Do you embrace traditional landscapes of order, or do you like natural landscapes? If you want a more natural look, be sure to research the regulations or landscape ordinances of your neighborhood or community first. Be prepared to get a variance and discuss what you are doing with your neighbors. Think about what you are capable of maintaining or how you plan to maintain your landscape. Landscape maintenance is a critical part of your scheme, so you must consider a plant's behavior and suitability for a particular landscape, be it formal or natural.

Yes, there are Midwest native plants that can be used traditionally; already most of our trees and some shrubs are embraced and readily utilized in landscaping, as are some ornamental grasses. But most native evergreen shrubs, vines, perennials, groundcovers, bulbs, and annuals are much less understood and cultivated. Some examples of those that have made the jump to "popular" include our native wisteria as a vine and prairie dropseed as a perennial.

Traditional styles where plants are grown in an orderly fashion show the hand of humans over nature. Plants usually must stay put and be segregated; only groundcovers are allowed to spread, and then only uniformly. Plants must be well behaved and under control. This is the typical style of suburbia, where shade trees, select ornamental trees, foundation plantings, hedges, and a few perennials prevail, adorning a lush, turf grass lawn.

Natural styles embrace the hands of Mother Nature and allow plants to naturalize freely and behave as they would in the wild. This allows for complex relationships and mixes of species that can look unkempt or untidy to many people. To the trained ecologist's eye, however, the pattern here is best described as "disordered hyperuniformity"—order at large distances, disorder at shorter distances. It's how plants are arranged in a native prairie.

There are in-between styles, the average perennial border being a good example, where relatively well-behaved plants are planted in groupings that create compositions that are usually synchronized for bloom through the seasons and in such a way so that the ornamental characters of the plant create artistic compositions based on color and texture. Piet Oudolf is a master of this design, and one can be inspired by his work at Chicago's Lurie Garden in Millennium Park.

Here's how I settled on a scheme for my landscape: I read the property restrictions of my subdivision and, luckily, leaving woodland and natural landscapes is allowed. I wanted a more orderly look immediately around the house and a more natural setting filled with wildlife beyond—that was why I moved to this semirural site. I retained a sweep of lawn around the house for access to maintain the house, for access to utilities, and as a place to walk and observe wildlife and the garden's plants. Though the Midwest is not in a major wildfire zone, I did keep that in mind, so the sweep of lawn could also act as a firebreak: I remember recent droughts and how areas of dried native vegetation can be explosive if on fire.

Besides being eye-catching, rattlesnake master is a great native neutral, here paired with purple coneflower at Chicago's Lurie Garden, Millennium Park.

My scheme also set parameters of function and aesthetics for the plants I chose. I already mentioned shade for the house during the hottest part of the day and winter windbreak. I didn't have any particular need for visual screens—be sure to look out all your windows, especially in winter and note what you see. I just worked to create beautiful edges to the existing woodland surrounding my home. I also knew my house created some more sheltered moist and shady microclimates on its north and east sides, where I could grow some plant treasures I enjoy without wasting resources. You never want to have to constantly baby plants for them to thrive.

When it came to aesthetics, I played with color and season of color. I chose a primarily orange-yellow-gold palette through the seasons for my west-facing front door entry space—a place I often sit and watch the sunset, so why not choose colors that play off that? For the hot, sunny, south side of the house, I chose bright red and vibrant purple, colors that invigorate. On the east side of the house, where I unwind and relax on the deck after work, the scheme is calming green foliage and white to pale flowers, which show up especially well at night; it's also where I have my best spring-flowering plants.

Follow your own choice of aesthetic schemes to make your landscape fit your needs and help give it some parameters, so that it is not all hodgepodge. The color palettes of our native plants through the season have their own splendor, whatever their original habitat. White, golden yellow, and lavender-purple are recurring color schemes of midwestern prairie plants. Clean, defined edges to natural landscaping along with signage are helpful for neighbors accepting of only a formal landscape. I certified my landscape with the National Wildlife Federation, North American Butterfly Association, and Monarch Watch and have posted the signs they provided. Other local and national groups will do the same, including Wild Ones and the Xerces Society.

You can also post your own signs—the idea is to communicate, somehow, what you are doing and what your natural landscape reflects.

Always embrace problematic site conditions. If you can't beat 'em, join 'em. A wet spot can become a wetland garden; a dry locale should embrace what does well in that habitat. Dense shade can usually support moss and ferns or other woodland wildflowers. Sandy sites have a whole suite of plants that thrive under those conditions. Make peace with what you are given, and a better, more sustainable design, unique to you and your site, will ensue. Capture your spirit of place and bloom where you're planted. There are native plants that thrive in every niche.

Garden Styles

Several garden styles lend themselves to incorporating native plants. Here we will look at prairie, woodland, water, and rock gardens, as well as edible landscapes.

PRAIRIE GARDENS

No other garden style provides more midwestern-appropriate, beautiful, and productive biomass to a landscape than a prairie garden, whether you are starting from scratch or adding to a remnant prairie, meadow, or grassland with existing natives. The most meaningful prairie gardens include only native plants found in the local area.

Prairie gardens provide exceptional food and cover for beneficial insects and wildlife. Virtually all are composed mainly of midsummer- to fall-blooming wildflowers, as the spring-blooming wildflowers are most costly to plant and challenging to establish. Prairie plantings also usually favor the larger warm-season grasses that are easier to establish. Smaller grasses like prairie dropseed and cool-season grasses like river oats get ignored, along with the many wonderful sedges.

A prairie planting is the epitome of a natural landscape, so must be planned and well thought out, particularly with regard to how it works with local landscape ordinances.

Its long-term maintenance must be carefully considered along with its flammability. In urban contexts, a landscape variance, clean edges, and signage are usually necessities. Burning is often not allowed, so an annual or occasional cut will be necessary. A flail mower is an ideal tool for cutting a prairie and chopping it into lovely mulch.

Almost all prairie gardens begin with a clean, weed-free plot in full sun. Plantings are most economical when started from seed, but using plant plugs can speed up the project. Select species for the planting mix that fit the site's soils whether sand, clay, or loam; wet, moist, or dry. Be careful with certain exuberant species: some may be integral but better added after more conservative species are established, so there is competition to keep them in check.

Your local native plant nursery will be able to recommend methods best suited to establishing a prairie garden in your particular area. I strongly suggest a mix of plugs and seed for smaller projects, starting with plugs or plants of some of the neglected spring wildflowers, smaller grasses, and sedges. Keeping weeds out through mowing high the first season or two also will help, while the long-lived prairie plants develop their roots. Black-eyed Susan and other short-lived, disturbance-dependent annual or biennial plants provide early color and suppress weeds; they will fade out as long-lived species become established. They will also prove to the uninformed that you aren't just tending a patch of weeds.

WOODLAND GARDENS

Beloved spring ephemeral wildflowers, spring-flowering trees, dazzling fall color, the promise of cool—all these are the inspiration for our common love of woodland gardens. They are a no-brainer for wooded landscapes. Just be sure to pick plants compatible with the types of trees and the environment you have.

Some gardeners in new, treeless landscapes want woodland gardens and that is not a problem either: start on the shaded north or east side of your home and plant trees that will eventually allow you to expand your woodland plantings. Most trees grow surprisingly fast when well sited and

Alumroots and wild indigos backed by the bright red spires of cardinal flower at the Greater Des Moines Botanical Garden.

A clump of Indiangrass underplanted with aromatic aster.

cared for, so refrain from choosing short-term, quick trees. I always recommend oaks and hickories. Oaks are more readily available at nurseries, but hickories can be grown from nuts that you collect, and they grow well in the shade, taking their time and being quite beautiful from seedling to sapling stage, with attractive buds and tropicalesque foliage. Some highly desirable small woodland trees, such as eastern redbud and pagoda dogwood, grow really fast and jumpstart your woodland garden.

One of the beauties of a woodland garden is that every type of plant is used to create the most complete, layered picture: canopy trees, understory trees, woodland shrubs, perennials, and so on. Vines must be carefully matched with young trees; you don't want them to smother their host, and they are best added to existing, more mature trees or against buildings or structures. Use fallen leaves for natural mulch, but don't let it get too thick until perennials are established. Surprisingly, most woodland wildflowers need bare earth to germinate, so you can rake away select spots or let foraging songbirds scratch through the leaf litter to open up new seedbeds.

Woodland gardens always have a focus on spring, but the other seasons must be included as well. Ferns have striking foliage that replaces spring ephemerals after they go dormant, and there are also some wonderful, if subtle, summer-blooming wildflowers, such as Culver's root and alumroot.

Fall in the woodland garden is often exuberant: various shade-loving asters and goldenrods create an outstandingly colorful display, with abundant nectar, pollen, and seeds for winter songbirds. Solomon's seal, false Solomon's seal, Jack-in-the-pulpit, and many other woodland plants have exquisite berries in late summer and autumn too.

Winter in the woodland garden should highlight some of our fine native evergreens, including Christmas fern and the stunningly patterned leaves of hepaticas.

WATER GARDENS

Claude Monet and his limpid paintings of water lilies popularized the water garden for eternity—not so surprising, given the beautiful subject. Water gardens are inherently intriguing. The sound of water, its exquisite reflective properties, its cooling nature, and the special suite of creatures it attracts make it a very popular garden type. Water plants are the showiest Midwest wildflowers, and many other lovely grasses and even more of our gorgeous wildflowers require wet feet.

Water gardens are not rain gardens; they must be sited out of major rainwater drainage, or they will quickly fill in with silt and debris. Obviously, they must be lined with soils that hold water or with a waterproof liner to be effective. Circulating water is needed for aeration, and filters are required to maintain water clarity, so gardens do not become cesspools. New construction styles pump water from below the pool so that it filters through gravel for purification and does not get clogged with leaves or other debris.

Design a water garden with various water depths for all sorts of plants, from those marginal plants that like wet feet to those that require a water depth of at least 18 inches. Water plants can be containerized and moved about, or even overwintered in the deepest parts of unheated pools, where the water doesn't freeze.

Water gardens with waterfalls, bubblers, and heaters that provide fresh water to wildlife and birds through all seasons are a naturalist's delight. There is no finer way to observe many of our colorful migrant songbirds, especially warblers, which relish drinking and bathing in such features.

Water is also a requirement for the life cycle of garden frogs and toads, whose peeps and trills are so welcome after a long winter; pools without fish or with shelves or nooks that fish cannot get to are best for these amphibians. Dragonflies and damselflies, a group of increasingly popular and dynamic insects, also require water for their eggs and juvenile life stages. Adult dragonflies and damselflies are wonderful predators of mosquitos and other nuisance insects, eating many of them on the wing.

ROCK GARDENS

Rock gardens, a garden fad of the 1920s, have lately seen a resurgence in popularity. They are ideal places to cultivate drought-tolerant native plants that grow wild on rock outcrops, cliffs, glades, talus slopes, and glacial deposits. Any landscape site with natural rock outcroppings is a likely place to try one. Rock gardens are also a good choice where steep changes of grade occur, and they can actually be living walls, where stones are dry stacked with a soil mix between them. Sharp drainage is essential for all rock gardens, though some rock garden plants thrive in wet scree or gravel.

When constructing a rock garden, use local stones and—crucially for aesthetics—set them in such a manner that they appear to be naturally occurring. Soil mixes between the rocks should be equal parts local topsoil, gravel, and compost. A gravel mulch can be applied to give a clean, neat look and to keep plants from rotting in wet weather.

Rock gardens that also function as retaining walls must have a sturdy footing and good drainage—that is, be backed by coarse gravel and drainage tile; this allows excess moisture to drain away and prevents frost heaving in winter. Each layer of stone on a living wall should be stepped back about ½ inch for buttressed support. The same soil mix should be placed between stone layers as recommended for any rock garden. An engineer should approve any wall taller than 4 feet to ensure that it is stable in the long term.

Plant living walls in spring; this gives the plants a chance to root in before summer's heat and, ideally, to be so well rooted by winter that frost heaving is not a concern. A mix of clay and sphagnum moss can be pressed around new plants to hold them in place as they establish.

EDIBLE LANDSCAPES

Edible landscaping, a concept first popularized by landscape designer Rosalind Creasy, simply means using food plants in the garden in a functional and aesthetically pleasing way, just as one would ornamentals. Gardeners and nongardeners alike have embraced both edible plants and edible landscapes, and these two trends have only gained momentum with the sustainability and foodie movements.

Foxglove penstemon, purple coneflower, and other Midwest native friends at the Greater Des Moines Botanical Garden.

The benefits of this garden style are the delicious treats produced by the plantings. Yes, there are native plants of all types, from shade trees to groundcovers, that are edible and should be valued for that reason. Pecans and highbush and lowbush blueberries are commercial successes. Other edible species are just as tasty but don't meet shipping or shelf life criteria, so are rarely found beyond local growers' and farmers' markets.

Incorporating native edibles into the home landscape definitely adds value to a sustainable garden, allowing one to celebrate and savor the bounty of the seasons. In my garden, I have edible shade trees from black cherries to persimmon, small trees of serviceberries and pawpaw, and riverbank grape vines, among others. Do I enjoy the food off these plants? You bet.

A collection of native food-yielding plants grown in a natural woodland manner is termed a *food forest*. Such a garden is both productive and ecologically sound. It's a good way to use many of the native edible plants that don't conform well to recommended planting and care for prime production; wild black raspberry plants, for instance, are too disease-prone to be cultivated in a formal, trained bed, but when allowed to run through open woodlands or woodland edges, there are always some that produce fruit to enjoy.

Nuisance Wildlife

Several creatures pose a major challenge to gardeners, and they have names that are four-letter words: deer, vole, and mole. Squirrels, rabbits, raccoons, woodchucks (groundhogs), gophers, and chipmunks are often problematic, too. When it comes to dealing with these creatures, there are no easy answers. Healthy gardens are simply habitat for native wildlife, and each owner will have to assess their own threshold of tolerance for the damage these creatures do to prized plants.

I do not call out deer-resistant plants in this book because a hungry deer will eat almost anything. I refuse to make plant choices based on these omnipresent and often overpopulated though beautiful creatures. I have fenced them out of part of my landscape and routinely use deterrent sprays elsewhere. I always support professional wildlife managers' decisions on their local control.

Historical records refer to the abundance of deer in the Midwest, and Lewis and Clark's journey supports that. I often hear people say we have built into their (deer) home, but that is not the real problem, as deer have adapted well to our suburban landscapes. These new "living lawn ornament" deer no longer fear being food for a wolf or cougar, so they are not on the move. They don't just browse a bit here and there and move on. They continually browse the same location, to the point that their favorite floral salads are exterminated.

Along with the recent expansion of agriculture into conservation reserve areas, the overpopulation of deer has become a top threat to our native plants and the creatures that rely on them—overtaking the bulldozer since the Great Recession. I have witnessed this firsthand on my own property, which was a deer park when I bought it: young oak trees all trimmed, not one redbud seedling, no violets, every aster eaten off before bloom. Now, sapling oaks have a chance to grow, violets have returned along with the fritillary butterflies, asters provide nectar to native pollinators in late summer and fall. My lone huge eastern redbud now has seedlings. This landscape rebirth is a result of fencing and deterring deer, though they are still a near-daily presence.

Weeding and Mulching

The most-time consuming maintenance in most gardens is the weeding out of tree seedlings. Nature often produces an abundance of elms, maples, and ash, to the point their seedlings can germinate almost in a carpet, and squirrels plant oaks, hickories, and walnuts. I try to think of it this way: removing tree seedlings (and other weeds) is just a garden chore that promotes physical fitness. I want my trees to be productive, as their fecundity is what creates such a rich web of life around me.

Most of our native perennials also readily self-sow in ideal conditions. It's what nature intended. If by chance you don't want seedlings, one option is to deadhead the plants (i.e., remove the seed heads), but that often ruins a plant's beauty, its winter interest, and its value to wildlife. Another option is plant perennials that don't produce copious seedlings.

Bare ground and light are what it takes to germinate most seeds, so a thick cover of plants with their natural duff and leaf litter really helps deter weeds, including many tree seedlings. I recommend mulch on new plantings in bare soil; it helps hold moisture and deter weeds until plantings are established. I am a member of what I call, tongue firmly in cheek, "mulch gardeners anonymous": I prefer to show plants, not mulch. But many homeowners still prefer plants tidily set in bare mulch; it's a very popular style, especially in traditional landscapes.

Mow your lawn with a mulching mower to efficiently recycle clippings. Mowers can be used to make passes over fallen leaves and grind them up in place rather than bagging them up and sending them to the landfill. Mulching and flail mowers can also be used on herbaceous plant borders.

I cart nothing off my own yard, running the mulching mower over excess leaves, chopping perennials in place, breaking up sticks. When disease- and storm-damaged trees had to be removed around the house, I had them chipped on site by the arborists, so that I could use the material for paths or mulch. Note: EAB-infested ash can be safely chipped and used for mulch, but certain diseased wood cannot be used that way, or you threaten to inoculate and infect new territory.

Bottle gentian in bloom, in a haze of little bluestem.

Garden-Worthy Midwest Native Plants

More than 6000 plants are native to the Midwest; the four plant profile chapters in this book present descriptions and photographs of the ones that are best for gardens in our region and suggest garden styles or landscapes for which the plant is most suited. The 225 featured plants are readily available at nurseries and have proven performance in cultivated landscapes. The general size of a plant is sometimes given, but keep in mind that many variables, from genetics to soils to available light, affect a plant's ultimate size. I have personally grown or widely observed all the plants in this book. My agenda is simply to educate gardeners and landscapers about our native plants and to inspire them to choose natives to create landscapes that are more relevant to our place.

Everyone reading this book has a different reason for wanting to grow native plants. Some will be more focused on restoring what has been lost; others may be more concerned with aesthetics. If your goal is to restore a native habitat, then use locally sourced plants from your ecoregion; these will have the genetics closest to what was once in your particular site. If your goal is a beautiful garden, utilizing a selected cultivar of a native plant may be best—one that is more adapted to your site's characteristics, has showier flowers or other ornamental attribute, or simply adds diversity to your landscape. My garden is a combination of these two goals: more formal and aesthetic selections around the house, but local strains in the woodland and prairie gardens.

Most native species are so adaptable that they do well over a wide range. Other plants are much more specific, and it is critical to use local strains. For example, when little bluestem plants sourced from the southern Ozarks are grown in the Upper Midwest, they are usually killed by frost before they even flower and set seed because the region's growing season is neither long enough nor hot enough for them. Likewise, some northern plant strains won't take the heat of the Lower Midwest: a northern-sourced roseshell azalea (*Rhododendron prinophyllum*) languished in the heat of my Lower Midwest garden, but an Ozark-sourced strain finally survived. Make sure to grow proven cultivars or local strains for your particular area of the Midwest, ones that still perform all the ecological functions of the wild plant—that is, pollinators still readily visit its flowers, caterpillars feed on its leaves, and so forth.

Trees

Allegheny serviceberry

Amelanchier laevis

woodland understory, woodland edges

full sun to part shade

When the ground has finally thawed across the American north, serviceberries burst forth with bloom as one of the first flowering trees. That's how they got their name: in earlier times, when serviceberries bloomed, graves for the deceased could finally be dug. This and other treelike serviceberries look great in woodland gardens; they are also suitable for formal landscapes, as they don't sucker or otherwise misbehave. Fall color can be one of the best: rich blends of warm yellow to apricot, orange to burnt red, and purplish red. Some plants have all these colors simultaneously, with leaves in full sun the reddest. This serviceberry bears the most succulent and delicious fruit of our midwestern tree species. Their delicious fruit makes them perfect in edible landscapes and food forests; birds find the berries just as delectable, making serviceberries integral in bird gardens.

The smooth, coppery new leaves of Allegheny serviceberry contrast exquisitely with its sparkling white flowers, giving this understory tree a rare beauty.

American arborvitae

Thuja occidentalis

Northwoods, moist forests

full sun to part shade

American arborvitae is a popular windbreak tree in the Upper Midwest. Its stunning foliage is rich in vitamin C, a hint as to why the name *arborvitae* ("tree of life") is so fitting. The tiny awl-type evergreen leaves are pressed to the twigs, which splay out into elaborate and undulating fan-shaped growth. The bark of old trees peels off into thin vertical strips of beige to whitish gray, adding to the tree's appeal. Cones are a favorite winter seed source for several finches, especially pine siskins. It makes a lush evergreen screen and is tolerant of light shade. Prefers moist, well-drained soils that are neutral to alkaline, often growing on or near wet sites with a constant supply of moisture but only where the roots are elevated. Intolerant of excessive heat and drought; be sure to shelter from summer wind and afternoon sun.

American arborvitae is a striking evergreen on Evening Island, Chicago Botanic Garden.

American hornbeam

Carpinus caroliniana

floodplains, woodlands

part to full shade

Here's a marvelous small ornamental tree for a shadier site, wonderful on the north or east side of a home or building, and a great native substitute for Japanese maple. It's hardy throughout the Midwest but needs proper siting away from hot, drying winds and scorching sun in the western portion of our region. American hornbeam is a beautiful addition under existing trees. Cultivate multitrunked trees to show off their fluted, muscular-looking bark. The ornamental trunks, smooth and bluish gray, are eye-catching in the winter landscape. The pendent, pagoda-like seed heads are light green and contrast well with the summertime foliage; they mature to brown and hang on the tree through winter. Fall color is one of the best, with shades from yellow and orange to scarlet, often all at once; a single specimen tree can glow like a flame, as the outer branches, which receive more light, have redder fall color.

American hornbeam is the perfect understory tree for a woodland garden.

American plum

Prunus americana

woodland and forest edges

full sun to part shade

The most widespread plum in the Midwest. The fragrant, white spring flowers with yellow anthers are iconic, blooming with redbuds in the Lower Midwest. The flowers, rich in nectar, are alive with pollinators and springtime butterflies. They bloom during neotropical migration in the Upper Midwest, so they often have orioles drinking from their blooms there. The fruits in early autumn are quite beautiful blends, from yellowish through rose with purplish tinge, and the leaves have good fall color, apricot yellow to red. Older trees develop nice bark with striking curled edges, and their gnarly form creates interest in the winter garden. Look for large cecropia cocoons on the tree in winter. All wild plums are tenacious, surviving in poor to rich soils as long as they are not continually wet. Trees are best suited to natural landscapes including sunny woodland borders and fencerows or the edges of food forests; they are open and weak in full shade.

American plums look as delicious as they taste.

apple serviceberry

Amelanchier ×grandiflora

woodland understory, woodland edges

full sun to part shade

The white flowers in early spring are a welcome sight after winter but are very brief, lasting only a few days in warm, windy weather. Serviceberries are among the first plants to fruit in early summer but are rarely messy, as birds quickly strip them. They are so relished by deer in my area that there is no chance of any plant surviving beyond their reach. Rabbits also savor these small trees as saplings, so tree guards, tree wrap, netting, or fencing is required as critter protection through winter. Self-sows on extremely rare occasions. The trunks are highly ornamental being smooth gray, developing dark striations of charcoal with full maturity. Apple serviceberry is a natural hybrid between the downy and Allegheny serviceberries, with many cultivars. One, 'Autumn Brilliance', selected in Illinois, does well throughout the Midwest and lives up to its name with consistent rich orange-red to purplish fall color.

Fall color on apple serviceberry is spectacular, with leaves in full sun being the reddest.

balsam fir

Abies balsamea

Northwoods

full sun to part shade

Balsam fir is the traditional American Christmas tree. The needles are aromatic, soft, dark green with a silvery underside. The cones are lovely blue-green and up-facing, disintegrating as they mature, leaving a toothpick-like center. The tight narrow crown of the tree is distinctive, but older, lower branches thin out with age. Balsam fir is a striking evergreen for a cool, afternoon-shaded site and works well in the sometimes-challenging north or east courtyards of homes and buildings. It can be used as a focal evergreen in appropriate cool-summer areas. Plant in moist, well-drained soils that are protected from hot afternoon sun and summer winds. Best in AHS heat zone 5 or cooler.

Balsam fir has a striking spirelike crown.

black cherry

Prunus serotina

successional lands, upland woods, fencerows

full sun to part shade

Consider planting black cherry in clumps and masses like river birch for a premier wildlife-friendly natural garden. Fruit is edible and makes a fine, bold-flavored juice. The lovely flowers, in bottlebrush-like clusters reminiscent of white lace, adorn the tree in midspring. The leaves host a wide variety of marvelous insects; it really is the epitome of a great bird plant beyond its fruit, which they also devour. Fall color—from golden yellow to apricot orange and scarlet often on the same tree—is among the best of any tree in the Midwest. Black cherry is long-lived and can thrive as an understory tree for many years. Mature trees readily grow 80–100 feet tall or more. Best in full sun but will grow in light or open shade. Well-drained soil is a must. Very heat and drought tolerant once established.

Its beautiful flaky bark has earned black cherry the nickname "potato chip tree."

blackhaw
Viburnum prunifolium

woodlands, forest edges

full sun to part shade

Blackhaw, a midland species, is one of three treelike viburnums that readily reach small tree size and stature in the Midwest; it grows with its northern and southern counterparts (nannyberry and rusty blackhaw, respectively) where their ranges overlap. All are usually suckering small trees that develop a main trunk and grow 20–35 feet tall at maturity. All are heat and drought tolerant once established. All will grow in light shade, but flowering will be heaviest in full sun. They are fine for large screens or as edge-of-the-woods plants and are occasionally used as focal ornamental specimens. Blackhaws are highly variable: some have a more treelike form of horizontal branches, reminiscent of a hawthorn; some display stunning red fall color. Tolerates a wide range of soils. Hardy throughout the Midwest.

The blue-black fruits of blackhaw are quite showy in fall and hang on the tree into winter.

bur oak

Quercus macrocarpa

floodplain forests, upland savannas, drier woodlands

full sun

Bur oak (named for its distinctive fringe-cupped acorns) is an iconic tree of the Midwest, gracing landscapes throughout our region. It is a magnificent tree, with a sculptural character that may exceed all other native shade trees, often displaying strong horizontal limbs that sweep to the ground. And it has tremendous wildlife value, hosting a wealth of insects and providing acorns for other creatures. Foliage is decidedly lighter underneath and is therefore quite beautiful in the wind; fall color is dull olive-golden-tan. Flowers appear as the leaves emerge in spring. Male flowers are pendent, gold-pollen-laden catkins; tiny female flowers produce the acorns. This prime shade tree grows 60–100 feet tall and wide and is resistant to wind, ice, and heavy snow, with a longevity of at least two centuries and often much longer. It is tolerant of urban conditions and a wide variety of soils, as long as they are not continually saturated. 'Big John' is upright and acorn-less.

This monumental specimen of bur oak, with a trunk diameter of 10 feet, grows near Columbia, Missouri.

chinkapin oak

Quercus muehlenbergii

floodplain forests, river bluffs, limestone outcrops

full sun

This marvelous long-lived shade tree is adapted to most street tree locations. It has deep coarse roots that are great for gardening beneath and aren't a menace to underground utilities. The tree's growth pattern translates into a gnarly crown of branching character that really stands out all winter. The light ashy gray bark is also quite noticeable. Fall color can be marvelous, from burnt orange into red tones. Chinkapin oak grows 50–80 feet tall and wide and prefers neutral to alkaline soils that are well drained, though it can be found in floodplain forests. Its native haunts suggest its adaptability to droughty conditions with urban concrete and rubble. It grows fast where happy, usually putting out a second flush of growth in summer.

Chinkapin oak, habit.

Chinkapin oak in bloom, showing its emerging leaves, which are easily identified by their characteristic sawblade-like teeth.

downy serviceberry

Amelanchier arborea

woodland understory, woodland edges

part to full shade

Serviceberries make ideal small trees (growing 15–30 feet) near a front entryway or around more intimate outdoor spaces. Most are multitrunked so can act as a perfect baffle screen between spaces. The more clumping and suckering types are not invasive and make good shrubs for back of the border, screening hedges, and edges of woodlands. Downy serviceberry is aptly named, scientifically, as it is the most arborescent (tree-sized) of the serviceberries. In most areas, downy serviceberry is simply a cloud of white in bloom, the woolly emerging leaves tiny at bloom time, not masking the early spring flowers whatsoever. This small tree is a common sight in the Ozarks in early spring and the only tree serviceberry in Missouri. The winter buds are thin and sharply pointed, more so than any other serviceberry. The trunks of mature trees are reminiscent of an old apple tree.

Downy serviceberry is nearly leafless when it sports its white flowers.

eastern hemlock

Tsuga canadensis

moist forests

part to full shade

Our most graceful evergreen, eastern hemlock has growth reminiscent of water cascading over a cone: from its nodding leader to the way the branches splay downward and outward like falling water. The green cones are cute, rarely more than 1½ inches long, maturing to brown. They adorn the branches through winter, when white-winged crossbills and many other songbirds gratefully feast on their seeds. Eastern hemlock is one of the few shade-tolerant evergreens, so it makes a great evergreen screen in moist, shady sites. It is also tolerant of shearing and makes a marvelous hedge. Not a good choice for prairie gardens. Plant eastern hemlocks in moist, well-drained soil, as they are intolerant of wet feet or too dry of a site. They need to be sited out of hot summer winds and to be shaded from the hottest afternoon sun. Plant only locally sourced, cold- and drought-tolerant trees in USDA zone 4 and much of the Western Midwest.

Eastern hemlock is shade tolerant in sheltered sites in the Midwest.

eastern hophornbeam

Ostrya virginiana

woodland understory

full sun to part shade

This stellar tree offers subtle four-season beauty. Pendulous golden male catkins appear in spring before leaves fully emerge; female flowers form pale green fruit that look like hops, mature to brown, and hang on the tree into winter. Cardinals and purple finch eat the seeds of the fruit. Fall foliage is golden brown, the leaves often persisting through winter; I've observed cedar waxwings settle in for the night, snuggled in the rich brown winter leaves. The delicate branching pattern is exquisite in winter, along with the rugged nature of mature trees and their finely longitudinal-striped bark. This species is a superior smaller shade tree for a confined space or under the canopy of other deciduous natives like oaks and hickories. Its winter leaves make it a good windbreak or winter screen in areas where an evergreen cannot be utilized. It's sturdy and long-lived in cultivation; a moist to seasonally dry, well-drained upland site is all that's needed. What kills our hophornbeam is compacted or poorly aerated, wet soils. Hardy throughout the Midwest.

Sturdy and long-lived, eastern hophornbeam bears clean, disease-free foliage throughout the growing season.

eastern redbud

Cercis canadensis

woodland edges

full sun to part shade

The spring-flowering trees of North America are almost universally white blooming—and then there's redbud, the state tree of Oklahoma. Spring bloom, before the tree leafs out, is this tree's most cherished aspect: tufts of flowers occur on the trunk and along every twig. Both the nectar-rich flowers and young pea pods are edible, so they are good plants for food forests and insectaries gardens. The light green pods become beautifully crimped as they mature, turning brown when ripe and adding interest as they hang on the tree in winter. Outside of polluted urban environments, the tree's trunk is cloaked in blue-gray and chartreuse lichens, and the bark of older trees often exfoliates to reveal reddish younger bark. Redbud loves our rich, calcareous soils, as long as they are not compacted and are well drained. It's at its best along the edges of woodlands or as the right-sized tree to grace an entryway, porch, deck, or patio. Recent Minnesota and South Dakota strains are hardy through USDA zone 4.

Eastern redbud's spring flowers are vibrant raspberry sherbet and equally refreshing—just what the doctor ordered after a long winter.

eastern red cedar

Juniperus virginiana

prairies, glades, disturbed open ground

full sun

Eastern red cedar is a premier evergreen windbreak and ornamental in challenging soils where other evergreens won't survive. It is a wildlife-friendly plant; female trees produce copious amounts of beautiful blue, berrylike cones that are relished by many birds, and it's also the sole host of our only green butterfly, the olive juniper hairstreak. Fruits are edible to a degree (juniper is the flavoring of gin); one in a thousand trees have sweet berries with a gin aftertaste. The foliage turns reddish brown or orangish olive in winter—beautifully in harmony with the hues of that season. Tree trunks are quite lovely, with whitish and tannish strips that exfoliate vertically, and often the trunk is adorned with white lichens. The plant thrives in any well-drained soil and does best in full sun; it is weak and open in light shade and does not survive in full shade. It is incredibly heat and drought tolerant and grows on rock outcrops with little soil. Hardy throughout the Midwest.

The beautiful blue "berries" of eastern red cedar.

Eastern red cedar enhances the springtime beauty of the Missouri Botanical Garden's Shaw Nature Reserve.

eastern white pine

Pinus strobus

Northwoods

full sun to part shade

This pine is the state tree of Michigan and a favorite tree of mine. The long, soft needles are in bundles of five (the five letters of *white* are often used to remind children how to identify it), the only Midwest native pine with that needle arrangement. Each needle has a whitened stripe down its underside, giving the tree a beautiful blue-green appearance overall. The needles capture the wind, generating a whispering rush like no other. Needles from the previous year turn rust brown and are shed annually in late summer, sometimes causing alarm to homeowners. Shed needles create fabulous and aromatic mulch under the tree. Mature trunks are charcoal black and ascend to the sky; horizontal limbs create a striking silhouette as the tree ages. Eastern white pine is the premier Midwest windbreak and screening tree, and a fine container plant as well. It grows best in moist, well-drained soils. Plants struggle in wet clay soils and during extreme dry spells but are overall the most widespread and adaptable of all our native pines.

Eastern white pine is widely planted across the Midwest.

flowering dogwood

Cornus florida

woodlands, rocky glades

full sun to part shade

This is the showiest of our native flowering trees by far, and the state tree of Missouri. Flowers are tiny yellowish clusters at the center of four milky white bracts; when viewed from below and illuminated by sunlight, they are unmatched. Fruits ripen in early fall, their scarlet red an advertisement to birds to disperse their seed. Fall foliage display is long-lasting and consistently showy; leaves develop purplish tinges after the autumnal equinox and turn pure red before dropping in late fall. The charcoal bark of old trees gets pebbly to reticulate. Flowering dogwood is a marvelous small tree for a woodland garden, woodland edge, or as a focal ornamental specimen in a traditional landscape. It's a must for a bird-themed garden; its fruits are rich in fats that fuel bird migration. Flowering dogwood requires well-drained soil. In areas with dogwood anthracnose, open locations with good air circulation are best. Afternoon shade is often beneficial in the western part of our region. Hardy through USDA zone 5b.

When in bloom, flowering dogwood is like a stunning white cloud of floating butterflies.

hackberry

Celtis occidentalis

floodplain forests, disturbed woodlands

full sun to part shade

Whenever the woodland hackberries are laden with fruit, I look forward to a birdie winter. Flocks and exceptional numbers of robins, bluebirds, waxwings, flickers, sap-suckers, and other fruit-eating birds visit, and the foliage hosts five species of butterflies. In summer there are two flights (early and late) of the most common butterfly in the region—the hackberry emperor—which remind me of the wildebeest of the butterfly world, as I can see hundreds in flight at a time. They overwinter as caterpillars rolled up in the fallen leaves so natural beds beneath the trees provide safe haven for them—lawn mowing and raking up leaves and debris spells their demise. The bark on young to middle-aged trees is furrowed with stunning corky warts, becoming shaggier with age. Fall color is yellow. Some strains make fine shade trees with a vase shape similar to its classic relative, American elm. Hackberry is incredibly adaptable to any soil but requires a warm summer; it is tolerant of heat, extreme cold, and extreme drought.

Here's an outstanding specimen of hackberry with a perfect vase shape reminiscent of an American elm.

honeylocust
Gleditsia triacanthos

floodplain forests, prairies

full sun

Give wild honeylocust a chance! The fierce branched spines that arm its trunk and stems provide protection for nesting songbirds. The finely textured leaves turn pure yellow in fall. The golden green female flowers, abuzz with pollinators, produce beautiful corkscrew pea pods; they are golden at first, almost black when mature, and rain down the lawn through winter. Seeded trees have value in food forests as a premier permaculture tree. The pods are edible, and the flowers produce nectar. Honey-locust indeed. Trees reach almost 100 feet at maturity, by which time some quit producing spines. Wild trees are treasured for wildlife gardens, as they are the sole host for a plethora of phenomenal moths, including two species of honeylocust silk moths, the moon-lined moth, the Magdalen underwing, and my favorite, the orange-wing—a moth that readily lands on people to imbibe sweat. Plant groundcovers and shrubs beneath wild trees to provide places for the pods to drop, along with cover for the overwintering moths. Honeylocusts are tolerant of urban soils and grow in tree wells set in concrete. Northern strains are hardy to USDA zone 4.

Pendent fruit adorns honeylocust's canopy.

hoptree

Ptelea trifoliata

woodlands, woodland edges, hedgerows

part to full shade

Here's a little tree more loved as a garden plant in Europe than in its heartland home. Plants are single-trunked but often low-branched, somewhat like an umbrella in form, with a rounded outer crown of foliage and open branching underneath. Hoptree is dioecious, with wonderfully fragrant tufts of creamy to golden light green flowers visited by many pollinators. Female plants are eventually adorned with waferlike fruit; light green in summer, they ripen brown and remain on the tree into winter. Hoptree readily naturalizes wherever planted, blurring the line between garden and wilderness. A must for a butterfly garden, it makes an ideal small tree for the natural garden or on the edge of woods; best in light shade. It's not for formal landscapes: giant swallowtail caterpillars are so numerous on my plants that they defoliate them and have even killed some plants because every leaf is repeatedly eaten. Very heat and drought tolerant.
Hardy throughout the Midwest.

The yellow-green flowers of hoptree are pleasantly fragrant.

Kentucky coffeetree
Gymnocladus dioica

floodplain forests

full sun to part shade

Don't be fooled by this ugly duckling, the coarser cousin of honeylocust; it becomes a swan as it matures. The foliage emerges coppery to purplish with silvered edges—beautiful in springtime but gorgeous when mature, thanks to the mesmerizing herringbone pattern of the leaflets; fall color ranges from rich to greenish yellow. Pale green flowers are pollinated by a few native bees. The rugged bark is stunning as it splits into plates that curl up on the edges—sharp enough to deter any would-be human climber (and probably a protective armor for long-extinct ground sloths). Kentucky coffeetree grows 60–100 feet tall and makes a fine shade and street tree; the light shade it casts and deep coarse roots mean you can even grow turf beneath it. It is amazingly wind- and ice-firm and also a premier home-shading tree, letting more passive solar sun through in winter. Tolerates a wide range of calcareous soils, as long as they are not wet for long periods. Somewhat shade tolerant. Hardy throughout the Midwest.

Kentucky coffeetree in the landscape.

nannyberry
Viburnum lentago

upland woods, wetlands

full sun to part shade

Nannyberry, the most wet tolerant of our three treelike viburnums, is distinguished by long-beaked, taupe winter buds. As with our other native viburnums (blackhaw and rusty blackhaw), showy clusters of white flowers with yellow stamens are produced with or soon after leaf emergence in spring. Berries turn lovely sage green when full-sized then gradually to pinkish and blue, ripening to a blue-black, drying on the tree, and holding into winter. The fruits are edible and taste a bit like a musky or bitter raisin. Fall color is good: some trees are uniformly red; others have exceptional blends from yellow to red.
The bark forms an interesting blocky texture with age. Thickets of the plant can spread 50 feet, making a fine large screen. Single-trunked specimens can be pruned into focal ornamentals. Tolerates a wide range of soils. Heat and drought tolerant once established. Hardy throughout the Midwest.

Nannyberry in beautiful bloom.

northern red oak

Quercus rubra

moist to dry upland woods

full sun to part shade

Northern red oak is another magnificent tree. It has a much higher crown than bur oak, atop a long dramatic trunk, but is not as tolerant of dryness or disturbed soils and is absolutely intolerant of the compacted soil left by construction activities. It is, however, our most shade-tolerant oak and a premier shade tree, 60–100 feet tall or more at maturity, very wind-firm and long-lived. The trunks are simply exquisite, with silvered bark striped by charcoal-colored fissures. Each fall, leaves turn everything from fine burnt reds to bronzed oranges and gold; purchase a tree while it's in fall color if you want a specific shade for your landscape. Flowers emerge in spring, with the leaves—golden male catkins and tiny female flowers that take two years to produce the distinctive large acorns, which have a relatively thin, flat-topped cap. Its acorns reliably provide excellent mast crops for wildlife, and the tree hosts a plethora of beneficial insects.

Northern red oak acorns.

A young northern red oak showing warm fall colors.

Ohio buckeye

Aesculus glabra

floodplain forests

full sun to part shade

Ohio's state tree leafs out early, a characteristic to be celebrated after a long winter. Its bright green palmate foliage is lit up even more by candles of nectar-rich green-yellow to yellow flowers, which are visited by bees, butterflies, hummingbirds, and songbirds like Baltimore and orchard orioles. The spring foliage and flowers are the perfect complement to blooming redbuds, an unforgettable pairing. Fall color is golden yellow to almost burgundy and blends thereof. The classic buckeye fruits that ripen in that season are a beautiful polished dark brown with a light brown "eye." The fallen nuts are quickly hoarded and literally squirreled away; they are poisonous to people but relished by squirrels. Often this otherwise ideal wildlife tree is the first to lose its leaves, which might be considered a drawback in a formal landscape, but specific trees or selections do hold their foliage well into autumn, so choose a local strain if this concerns you. A great choice for a woodland garden, or as a small shade or understory tree. Hardy throughout the Midwest.

Ohio buckeye's distinctive foliage and flowers.

Ohio buckeye in full bloom at Chicago's Montrose Point Bird Sanctuary.

pagoda dogwood

Cornus alternifolia

moist woodlands

full sun to part shade

A fine ornamental tree for a wooded landscape. Its most beautiful attribute is present year-round: its distinctive horizontal branches, which curve upward at the ends (hence the common name). Clusters of creamy white flowers are set above clean foliage in late spring. Fruit ripens bluish black in late summer. Leaves turn yellow to burgundy-red in fall. Pagoda dogwood is a premier bird garden plant; its berries, high in lipids, are relished by an array of songbirds and are certain to attract new species to your yard. It is also useful at the corner of a house, where it softens harsh edges, and it is exquisite in and on the edge of a wood. It demands well-drained soils and struggles in heavy clay or compacted soil. It will grow in full sun in a moist, sheltered site but prefers high shade and protection from hot afternoon sun; even in the Upper Midwest, it will languish in a hot dry site. Two trees are needed for good fruit set. Hardy throughout the Midwest.

Pagoda dogwood grows fast when young, adding a new tier of horizontal branches each season.

Pagoda dogwood flowers in late spring.

paper birch
Betula papyrifera

prairies, wetlands, woodland edges

full to part sun

No tree is more beloved for its stunning white bark than the paper birch. The bark is like that of no other native tree, peeling off into smooth plates with contrasting black horizontal lenticel scars. A tree in spring is draped in golden catkins, and fall color is consistently a rich yellow. Paper birch makes an exquisite mass planting along the edges of woodlands. Though it becomes a shade tree, it is often grown by nurseries in clumps to show off its beautiful bark. It does make a nice focal planting and is a fine tree to plant near an outdoor seating area, where night lighting will reflect off its trunks. The tree has very high wildlife value as host to many moths, and its seeds are relished by finches in winter, especially the redpolls that winter in the Upper Midwest from the Arctic. Paper birch requires well-drained soil and at least very high light; it prefers the cooler and more moist Upper Midwest.

A stand of paper birch highlights the wildflower garden at the Minnesota Landscape Arboretum.

pawpaw

Asimina triloba

floodplain forests, alluvial woods, dry upland woods

full sun to part shade

The large leaves of this little tropical-looking tree are its most handsome aspect: smaller and droopy in sun, larger and held horizontally in shade to capture available light, illuminating their character. Spectacular fall color, yellow to white-yellow. The spring flowers look like purple trilliums: maroon-purple with three petals. Pawpaw's edible fruits ripen in early fall. Eat only ripe fruit and harvest as soon as it is ready, or raccoons and opossums will beat you to them. Pawpaw can be a focal ornamental in full sun, where it forms a dense pyramidal tree. It's also lovely as a thicket-forming grove in a shade garden. It's an essential plant for a food forest or an edible landscape. It's also integral to a butterfly garden as the only host plant of the zebra swallowtail butterfly, the sole hardy member of the tropical kite swallowtails. It requires rich soil. Amazingly heat and drought tolerant once established. Select varieties are grown for superior fruit; two different cultivars are required for fruit set. Hardy to USDA zone 5.

Pawpaw's distinctive edible fruits.

pecan
Carya illinoinensis

alluvial plains

full sun

Lush green foliage—through the hottest and driest seasons and through record floods—is the beauty of a pecan tree. The ashy, light gray bark, with intricate shagginess, is also beautiful upon close inspection. After the flavorful, oil-rich nuts have fallen, the blackened husks, which linger on a bare tree into winter, are quite ornamental. Pecan becomes a premier and magnificent shade tree, 80–100 feet tall. It's a perfect choice for natural landscapes, edible landscapes, nut orchards, and food forests. These trees are tolerant of a wide range of soils and have amazing heat, drought, and flood tolerance. Late freezes or extreme cold can damage flower buds, inhibiting nut production. Specialty nurseries sell local cultivars selected for better nut quality; trees require cross-pollination with an appropriate cultivar for fruit set. Hardy throughout our region, and lately, the growing season even in the Upper Midwest has been long enough and warm enough for nuts to ripen: the Minnesota Landscape Arboretum had its first pecan harvest in 2017.

A luxuriant pecan tree at the Chicago Botanic Garden.

Pecan's intricately shaggy bark adds interest to the winter garden.

persimmon

Diospyros virginiana

diverse habitats

full sun to part shade

Persimmons usually serve as small shade trees, but they readily reach 50 feet or more at maturity. The stunning blocky bark, like an alligator's hide, shows best in winter. The early summer flowers are small white urns little noticed among the foliage, but when in bloom, trees are abuzz with bees. Female trees produce delicious edible fruit, sweet when ripe; they'll give you a memorable puckered mouth if eaten too early. Persimmon is thus a great food forest tree, and select female clones with larger, tastier fruits are available from specialty nurseries. Female trees finally drop their fruit in winter, creating a messy situation for tidy landscapes, but they are a boon to wildlife and make a welcome addition to a natural garden. Do not plant near native prairie remnants: persimmon's tenacious roots resprout prolifically. Best in full sun, tolerant of soils from periodically wet to dry. Amazingly heat and drought tolerant once established. Hardy to USDA zone 5.

Besides being sweet and tasty, persimmons can be quite beautiful when they are peachy yellow and ripe, right after fall leaf drop.

pin oak

Quercus palustris

floodplain forests, upland flatwoods

full sun

Pin oak is far superior to current widely planted non-native trees and now dominates Lower Midwest urban forests, eventually reaching 60–100 feet tall. Wildlife value is extremely high: it supports a plethora of insects, and its heavy mast of small acorns are relished by songbirds. It is a premier shade tree in locations with room for its skirt of lower branches, which—if allowed to sweep to the ground—create a natural children's play space or fort. Young trees hold their leaves through winter, serving as a good screen and windbreak for a couple of decades or more. Pin oak also makes a good street tree; it's often used to line entrance drives, making a grand impression when branches over the drive are pruned up while outer branches are allowed to cascade. Rich clay to loam soils that are neutral to acidic are a must; it turns an anemic yellow in alkaline soils, and it's not happy in rubble fill or where the earth has been sculpted for development. Hardy throughout the Midwest.

Pin oak's fall color is brilliant burnt red to scarlet in cooler autumns.

quaking aspen

Populus tremuloides

successional lands, open ground

full sun

Quaking aspen is best known for its pure yellow fall color. Trees are narrowly upright, usually growing in tight groves. The trunks are very showy, grayish white to white with black horizontal markings. The rounded leaves wobble in the slightest breeze on their thin, flattened petioles, giving quaking aspen its scientific and common names; their trembling creates a pleasant sound and adds sparkling movement to the landscape. It's a memorable ornamental shade tree, particularly when allowed to grow into a naturalistic clump or grove; it makes a fine summer screen, especially good for buffering noise. Quaking aspen does best in areas with cooler summers (AHS heat zone 6 and cooler); it will grow southward in moist, sheltered locations.

The bark of quaking aspen is reminiscent of paper birch but does not exfoliate.

Quaking aspen in the landscape.

red maple

Acer rubrum

moist to wet forests

full sun to part shade

Probably the most widely cultivated tree in the Midwest and a fine shade or street tree. Homeowners have embraced it for its quick growth rate and gorgeous fall color, from red or burgundy to orange and muted yellow—be sure to select a tree in that season so you can pick the color you want. The underside of the leaf is a lighter color, which enhances the tree's overall appearance. Flowers are tiny, yellow to ruddy red; they are borne in early spring before the tree leafs out and are a good source of nectar and pollen (male flowers) for early pollinators. The helicopter seeds on female trees are pale salmon to showy red. Red maple grows 50–80 feet tall. Try it in a rain garden, a moist woodland garden, or at the edge of a water garden. It appreciates soils with lower pH and suffers in the Western Midwest, often becoming chlorotic yellow, with scorched leaves in summer and severe sunscald on the trunks.

Red maple leaves in brilliant fall color.

river birch

Betula nigra

floodplain forests

full sun to part shade

When young, river birch has gorgeous exfoliating bark that curls into papery sheets, revealing planes of cream, salmon, and cinnamon beneath. The winter tracery of twigs tipped by catkins is subtly beautiful, and the golden bloom of the catkins, before trees leaf out in early spring, deserves appreciation, too. It becomes a large shade tree over time; bark on older trunks is dark charcoal-gray, and the crown of mature trees often cascades all around the edges, with lovely weeping branches. Fall color is sometimes a good yellow. It is commonly cultivated in clump form, as a focal ornamental tree, but shows best planted in groves. Its water-seeking surface roots compete well with turf. Most cultivated river birches are cultivars selected for exceptional bark characteristics; Heritage ('Cully') is the most widely grown. River birch can suffer iron chlorosis (yellowing) and even die in soils with a high pH. Thus it is not recommended for street tree use, where alkaline concrete and rubble are in the soil. Hardy through the Midwest.

River birch in the landscape.

rusty blackhaw
Viburnum rufidulum

wooded slopes, forest edges

full sun to part shade

Rusty blackhaw is our southern treelike viburnum and a great plant for screening or the woodland edge, offering year-round interest: showy white flowers in late spring, good fall color, and the ripe blue-black berries are held on the tree into winter. Single-trunked specimens can be pruned up as little trees. Rusty blackhaw is distinguished by its rusty, dark brown winter buds and exceedingly lustrous, almost lacquered leaves. Tolerates a wide range of soils, thrives in any well-drained soil, and is extremely heat and drought tolerant once established. Flowers best in full sun. Hardy to USDA zone 5.

The polished leaves of rusty blackhaw turn flaming red in the fall.

sassafras
Sassafras albidum

open deciduous forest, forest edges

full sun

Sassafras has a beautiful winter silhouette, with young stems and twigs decidedly green (it actually was used as a substitute Christmas tree before evergreens were planted on the prairies). In spring, greenish yellow flowers stud the upturned branch tips before the elegant leaves emerge, another perfect complement to blooming redbuds. Extraordinary fall colors—yellow, orange, red, purplish—all often present on a single tree. Female trees produce distinctive fruit—a bluish black berry set on a succulent red pedestal, somewhat like a golf ball on a tee, designed to be seen by birds against the green foliage. Sassafras makes an amazing shade tree or grove in a more naturalistic land-scape, well over 50 feet tall at maturity. It's a good bird and butterfly garden plant: the late summer fruits are relished and dispersed by songbirds, and it's one of only two host plants for the spicebush swallowtail. Sassafras takes to just about any well-drained soil. Tenacious where present, usually suckering into a grove. Hardy to USDA zone 5b.

Sassafras leaves in all three shapes—simple, mitten (one lobe), and ghost (two lobes)—show well when backlit by the sun.

scarlet oak

Quercus coccinea

moist forests

full sun

This species has not only the best red fall color of our oaks but some of the finest fall color of *any* shade tree, in glowing scarlet red. There is something almost other-worldly about a scarlet oak in peak fall color. Its name says a lot, but the translucency of the leaves capturing the low sunlight of autumn, combined with the intense saturated color, is simply stunning. Scarlet oaks require well-drained acidic soils (they suffer from chlorosis in alkaline conditions) and are fussy about being transplanted. They make fine shade trees, 50–60 feet tall, and are best isolated as specimen trees, not planted in groves. Works well in a natural landscape. Produces abundant smaller acorns relished by wildlife.

shagbark hickory

Carya ovata

oak-hickory forests

full sun to part shade

Shagbark hickory usually grows 60–90 feet tall. The bark on mature trees is absolutely beautiful; it splits off in flat gray strips that bend outward from both their upper and lower ends. Equally ornamental are the scarlet scales of emerging leaf buds, which unfurl like petals of a flower surrounding the splendid form of the emerging compound leaves. Fall color is yellow to golden brown. A fine shade tree for edible landscapes and food forests. Young trees are tolerant of all but dense shade but grow best in full sun; they make striking specimens, their large leaves contrasting nicely with other vegetation. Why would anyone want a Japanese maple instead? The nuts are delicious and nutritious. Shagbark hickory is extremely drought tolerant, surviving in almost any well-drained soil. Hardy throughout the Midwest.

Scarlet oak has the most vibrant red fall color of any oak.

The shaggy bark of shagbark hickory is without equal.

shingle oak

Quercus imbricaria

successional lands

full sun

Shingle oak holds its leaves through winter for up to 50 years, making it a wonderful windbreak and screen in soils or situations where evergreens won't grow. Fall color may be red on saplings, but small to large trees simply turn brown late in fall. The tree starts out with pyramidal growth—somewhat like a pin oak but with less-pendent branches—and matures at nearly 100 feet tall and just as wide in good soils, with a large rounded crown. It makes a fine street and shade tree, with abundant tiny acorns relished by wildlife. Shingle oak grows very fast and tolerates disturbed soils. It is one of our shortest-lived oaks, fully mature and declining by age 100. Hardy throughout the Midwest, but northern strains must be grown in USDA zone 4.

Shingle oak creates beauty in the landscape.

sugar maple
Acer saccharum

moist forests

full sun to part shade

This is the state tree of Wisconsin and the inspiration for the iconic leaf on Canada's flag. Some trees display spectacular fall color, from brilliant reds to orange and yellow. In spring the tree is cloaked in pendent chartreuse flowers before it leafs out—what a complement above a carpet of spring wildflowers. It and beech are our most shade-tolerant trees, fast increasing in the understory as woodlands become closed forests. Sugar maple casts dense shade and has dense surface roots, so limits turf beneath it when mature. It can be planted in food forests, but a tree should be 50 years old before tapping for sap. A fine shade tree, perfect for a woodland garden or other moist, upland soil sites. Sugar maples grow 50–80 feet tall and are highly variable; local strains are a must, especially in the western part of our region, where northern-sourced plants languish and die prematurely during hot, dry summers.

Sugar maple, in peak fall color, is one of our most beloved native shade trees.

swamp white oak
Quercus bicolor

floodplains, sandy wetlands, upland flatwoods

full sun

Swamp white oak, the darling of city foresters, is easy to grow in urban-damaged soils: about 400 of these trees grace the World Trade Center Memorial in New York City. This tree has an upright oval crown when young, with a skirt of drooping branches, but as it matures, its shape becomes broad-spreading. An open-grown swamp white oak is a sight to behold, with magnificent horizontal limbs. It usually grows 60–80 feet tall and wide. The two-toned leaves sparkle as their undersides show in a breeze, and when night-lit, the swamp white oak literally shines, as the undersides of its leaves reflect light. A premier shade tree, but it's for neutral to acidic soils only: swamp white oak suffers chlorosis in areas where soils are limey and alkaline. Do not plant in soils with a high pH.

tulip tree
Liriodendron tulipifera

moist forests

full sun

Tulip tree, the state tree of both Indiana and Kentucky, grows like a rocket skyward and lives on for centuries. Young greenish trunks are striped and speckled with white. The distinctively shaped leaves turn a rich yellow in fall. Flowers are also special, being light green with a flame of orange and yellow at the base of each "petal" surrounding a central golden cone. Flowers are often unseen; they bloom after the leaves emerge in late spring and are often high in the tree. Blond, conelike fruits adorn the tree in winter. This monstrous shade tree, reaching 80–120 feet tall or more, is suitable for large gardens. It's very beautiful planted en masse, where its straight trunks quickly create cathedral-like columns with a shady space for woodland garden plants beneath. Tulip tree requires rich, moist soils that are never wet for any period of time. Saplings grow quickly provided they have sun. Hardy to USDA zone 5; a few stunted trees survive in sheltered sites in zone 4.

Swamp white oak has dark green leaves with strikingly whitened undersides.

Tulip tree's flowers are beautifully colored but rarely noticed high in the leafy canopy.

white oak
Quercus alba

moist to dry woodlands

full sun to part shade

White oak, the state tree of Illinois, is known for its beautiful and uniform branching, stout (wider-than-tall) crown, and consistently stunning fall color. Young leaves are silvery, and young trees often hold their foliage into winter. This premier oak, like all oaks, has a high wildlife value, thanks to its acorns, and makes a fine, long-term shade tree. It grows 50–100 feet tall. White oak abhors construction-damaged, compacted, or otherwise destroyed soils. Plant it in well-drained soils that are moist to summer dry and have not been graded or filled. In appropriate soils, it actually grows surprisingly fast, with two flushes of growth per summer season. Next to the northern red oak, it's our most shade-tolerant native oak.

The exquisitely curved, deeply lobed leaves of white oak paint the fall with a range of warm colors.

white spruce
Picea glauca

Northwoods

full sun to part shade

The full, pyramidal form of white spruce is highly desirable in home landscapes; the needles are more bluish green than other evergreen trees, creating a nice contrast. The cones are small and often abundant, adding winter interest; they produce copious amounts of seeds that attract winter songbirds. A prime evergreen for a windbreak or focal ornamental. Older trees often lose their lower branches, especially if shaded or in stressful locations. White spruce requires moist, well-drained soils and can suffer in the hot, humid Lower Midwest. Thankfully, virtually all the white spruces in Midwest nurseries are derived from the South Dakota form (aka Black Hills spruce).

A mature *Picea glauca* 'Densata', a South Dakota form that is better adapted to hotter, drier parts of the Midwest, at historic Vaile Mansion in Independence, Missouri.

yellow birch
Betula alleghaniensis

maritime to drift plains, in moist, cool ravines

full sun to part shade

The trunks and limbs of this tree are its chief ornamental attribute, featuring silvery to coppery gray exfoliating bark. The crushed buds and stems give off a strong scent of wintergreen, and I can't resist sampling them every time I meet the tree. Fall color shows rich yellows. Yellow birch makes a fine shade tree in a moist sheltered site. Plant it on the north or east side of a home to mimic the cooler microclimates it inhabits in nature. It is a fine woodland garden tree, and it displays nicely when planted in clumps or masses. The tree should definitely be included in food forests: it contains oil of wintergreen, used for flavoring root beer and other brews and comestibles. Yellow birch is tolerant of more shade than our other birches but does best in full sun. Make it at home by siting it in a rich, moist soil that is well drained.

Yellow birch has subtly but sublimely beautiful bark.

Shrubs

Adam's needle yucca

Yucca filamentosa

uplands

full sun to part shade

Adam's needle yucca can be used in harsh sites and sunny, windswept, rocky landscapes where many evergreens would struggle. Its large flower spike reaches above the spiky basal leaves, forming a spectacular 4- to 6-foot tall candelabrum of white flowers in early summer. It was these glowing flower spikes, along with the fact that Adam's needle yucca was often planted in cemeteries, that inspired the nickname "ghosts in the graveyard." Where its pollinating yucca moths are present, Adam's needle yucca produces seedpods that hold well into winter. It grows in almost any upland soil from clay to sand, has a tenacious root that is nearly impossible to remove, and even survives in light shade, though it doesn't flower in shade.

The flowers of Adam's needle yucca gleam in the intense light of early summer.

American elderberry

Sambucus canadensis

moist woodland and forest edges, roadsides

full sun to part shade

American elderberry is a fine plant for natural landscapes, bird gardens, edible landscapes, and food forests. The huge, flat clusters of lacy white flowers are gorgeous and often rebloom into summer, finally becoming abundant displays of fruit that ripen to dark purplish black and are attractive in late summer into fall. Mature shrub size is 8–15 feet, usually with multiple stems, although some specimens are almost treelike. The fruit (and flowers) are edible, making excellent jellies, syrups, and preserves (but note: stems and foliage are highly toxic). Elderberry is rich in antioxidants and used by some as a nutritional supplement. It's easy to divide and grows fast but does require well-drained soil and full sun to only part shade to flower and fruit well. Hardy throughout the Midwest.

When the greens of June cloak other plants, American elderberry bursts forth with white dinner plates of flowers. No native shrub blooms so spectacularly through summer's solstice.

American hazelnut

Corylus americana

prairies, savannas, oak-hickory forests

full sun to part shade

Yes, this is the native counterpart to the hazelnuts sold in grocery stores, with very similar, though smaller, nuts. It's often the first plant to bloom in spring, with tiny female flowers that look like fuchsia spiders and handsome golden catkins that drape abundantly from the twigs. Bracts that encase the nuts turn light green in summer, contrasting with the dark green leaves. Fall color is one of the best, the leaves turning orange to red. This lightly to strongly suckering shrub gets larger than often attributed, readily growing 12 feet tall; the champion in Washtenaw County, Michigan, is an astounding 35 feet tall and wide. The plant is best in natural and wildlife-themed gardens, natural area restorations, edible landscapes, and food forests. Bees relish its pollen, and it is a favorite browse for rabbits and deer as well as many species of caterpillars that feed on related birches. American hazelnut tolerates any well-drained soil in full sun to light shade. Hardy throughout the Midwest.

American hazelnut once formed dense thickets across the Midwest and is best used in a natural garden, where it can spread.

American highbush-cranberry

Viburnum opulus var. *americanum*

moist woodlands

full sun to part shade

American highbush-cranberry is a more shrublike viburnum but may have tree-sized stems. It's named for its vibrant red berries that hold their color through subzero weather—a rare hot note in a bitter cold, snowy landscape. Winter birds such as cedar waxwings seek the fruit in wintertime after the berries have frozen and thawed and probably fermented. Fruit is edible, but very tart; flowers are a stunning white, and the foliage is an elegant, three-pointed lobed leaf, reminiscent of a maple. Fall color is noteworthy, ranging from yellow to red and burgundy-purple on sun-exposed foliage. A magnificent 8- to 12-foot large shrub of upward branches that arch outward, this viburnum makes a good back-of-the-border or edge-of-the-woods plant, or can stand alone as a stunning ornamental. It can grow taller, with fewer stems reaching for light, in woodland gardens. Readily takes to moist, well-drained soils throughout the Midwest but must be in shaded, cooler sites on the north or east sides of buildings in AHS heat zones 6 and 7.

The lacecap flower of American highbush-cranberry stands out against the fresh foliage of late spring.

black chokeberry

Aronia melanocarpa

sandstone cliffs to wetlands

full sun to part shade

Chokeberries are all the rage now. Their dark fruit is edible and rich in antioxidants; the berries don't make one choke, but they do have a memorable aftertaste. They make excellent preserves reminiscent of cherries, and juice from the fruit is increasingly added to juice blends. Black chokeberry grows 3–5 feet tall, is tidy and well behaved, and makes a great ornamental shrub for a traditional garden. The foliage and flower stems are smooth and glossy on most forms. The leaves turn rich saturated shades of red in the fall. Black chokeberry produces clusters of showy white flowers with pink stamens that are presented well as they are set above the leaves. The fruit is inky black when ripe, often beautifully polished in fall, and creates a striking contrast to the red fall leaves. The dried fruit remains on the plant all winter. Black chokeberry can be cultivated in a wide range of soils from sand to clay.

Black chokeberry makes an attractive small shrub for a traditional landscape.

dwarf indigobush

Amorpha nana

upland prairies

full sun

Dwarf indigobush is another premier native that is worth seeking out, one that will add both beauty and wildlife value to your yard. In early summer, spikes of indigo-purple flowers with contrasting golden stamens cover this deciduous landscape shrub, which rarely grows more than 2 feet tall. The pinnately compound leaves are green and finely textured; they have translucent glandular dots, which you can see by holding them between you and the sun. Tiny legume pod fruits adorn the plant into winter. Dwarf indigobush blooms only from old wood; if you cut it back, it will not flower until the following growing season. In a garden setting, just about any well-drained soil will make it happy. Hardy throughout the Midwest.

Dwarf indigobush produces beautiful flowers in early summer.

fragrant sumac

Rhus aromatica

uplands, limestone outcrops

full sun to part shade

Fragrant sumac's tiny yellow flowers are relished by the first insects of spring, their bloom coinciding with the emergence of the spring azure butterfly. Female plants produce stunning red, fuzzy fruit that ripens from late spring into midsummer, when they are one of the most ornamental features of any plant, contrasting perfectly with the green foliage. Fruit becomes dark reddish brown by late summer and occasionally persists into winter. Fall color is exceptional on plants originating locally or regionally. Winter twigs, tipped with next spring's flower buds, are a favored browse of deer and rabbits. Larger forms of this popular shrub are occasionally used as focal ornamentals but are mainly seen at the back of the border or as screen plants; smaller cultivars ('Gro-Low', for example) are used as groundcovers. The edible fruits have become trendy for flavorings and teas and are in demand by chefs working with local ingredients. Fragrant sumac grows best in well-drained, limestone-based soils, from pure sand and gravel to clay. Hardy throughout the Midwest.

Fragrant sumac in the landscape.

gray dogwood

Cornus racemosa

successional lands, woodland edges

full sun to part shade

Gray dogwood is another thicket-forming shrub, with smooth, flat leaves. Where I grew up, it harbored the marvelous thumping dance of the ruffed grouse, which (like various resident and migrant songbirds) relishes its lipid-rich berries. This plant has the same niche, cultural requirements, and landscape use as roughleaf dogwood—making a fine screen or hedgerow plant—but is more tolerant of wet soils. Its fall color is more burgundy to purple with a polished leather look to the leaves, and it is finer and of smaller stature than roughleaf dogwood. Hardy throughout the Midwest.

The white autumn berries combined with burgundy fall color make gray dogwood a standout in that season.

highbush blueberry

Vaccinium corymbosum

open swamps, bogs

full sun to part shade

Highbush blueberry is a nonsuckering shrub that usually grows 4–6 feet tall in the Midwest, but it can become a large shrub 8 feet tall and over 10 feet wide. Many cultivars of highbush blueberry have been cloned for their superior fruiting traits and are widely cultivated for fruit production, especially in western Michigan. Their fruits are the typical blueberries found in grocery stores, and birds appreciate them just as much as we do. A fantastic shrub for edible landscapes, food forests, and as an ornamental specimen in traditional landscapes. Be sure to give highbush blueberry acidic organic soil; it may be easier to provide this in a raised bed.

Highbush blueberry's beautiful fall color is the equal of any ornamental shrub.

Kalm's St. John's wort

Hypericum kalmianum

sand prairies, sand savannas, sandy lakeshores

full sun to part shade

Kalm's St. John's wort, a Great Lakes endemic, is nonetheless easy to cultivate in almost any well-drained soil. The foliage is small, narrow, and long, creating a fine texture, often bluish green and turning shades of yellow, orange, and red in fall. The flowers cover the plant in midsummer as a mass of yellow, with abundant bushy stamens; they are rich in pollen and visited by frenzied pollen-collecting bees. The seedpod fruits mature brown and adorn the plant through winter. The bark too is attractive, exfoliating to show mahogany tones underneath. Kalm's St. John's wort grows just 3–4 feet tall and makes a fitting low hedge, foundation plant, or shrub mass. It is relatively short-lived but self-sows sparingly.

Kalm's St. John's wort is an adorably small, tidy shrub for a traditional landscape.

leadplant

Amorpha canescens

upland prairies and savannas

full sun to part shade

Leadplant was common above the lead mines of the Driftless Area, which is how it got its common name. Its early summer flowers are dark indigo with contrasting yellow-orange stamens; they are set in up-facing, multibranched spikes atop finely textured gray pinnately compound leaves. The flowers produce clusters of little legume pod fruits, which adorn the plant into winter. Leadplant rarely grows more than 3 feet tall but can be maintained as a 30-inch-tall herbaceous perennial. The shrub grows in almost any well-drained soil in full sun or no more than morning shade. It is extremely heat and drought tolerant, very long-lived once established, and easy to maintain by pruning in late winter or early spring. Leadplant blooms on new wood, so it can be cut back in winter and will flower by midsummer. Hardy throughout the Midwest.

Leadplant is another tidy plant, suitable for a traditional border, as depicted here at Powell Gardens, Missouri.

lowbush blueberry

Vaccinium angustifolium

rocky upland woods, sand dunes, prairies, savannas

full sun to part shade

Lowbush blueberry usually grows just 18 inches tall and spreads slowly into a thicket. Its fruits are often marketed as wild blueberries, as the species is seldom cultivated commercially for fruit production, though wild stands are harvested. Its smaller blueberries are considered more flavorful than most highbush blueberries. The many hybrids (both man-made and naturally occurring) between highbush and lowbush blueberries display improved hardiness, larger berries, and more productive fruiting; most are from Minnesota and have "north" or northern places in their names. These highbush-lowbush or "half-high" hybrids have proven garden-worthy south into USDA zone 6, AHS heat zone 7.

Blueberries are beautiful on lowbush blueberry and delicious to eat.

New Jersey tea

Ceanothus americanus

upland prairies and savannas

full sun to part shade

New Jersey tea makes a tidy low shrub 2–3 feet tall suitable for a traditional landscape or wildlife garden. The white clusters of midsummer bloom are very showy and attract a wide array of pollinating insects. The flowers produce seed capsule fruits that turn black as they ripen and explode when fully ripe; capsule remnants may remain on the plant into winter, adding interest. New Jersey tea thrives in rich, well-drained soils. Once established, it is very long lived and can easily be maintained by late winter or early spring pruning. It blooms on new growth, like an herbaceous perennial.

Frothy white clusters of flowers adorn New Jersey tea on Harlem Hills Prairie, Winnebago County, Illinois.

ninebark

Physocarpus opulifolius

moist woodlands, wetlands

full sun to part shade

Ninebark is one of the finest large screening and hedge plants, capable of becoming a very large shrub, 8–12 feet tall and eventually wider than tall. It's beautiful on the edge of a woodland but usually too open and sparse in a shade garden. It blooms in late spring after the leaves emerge, its clusters of nectar-rich white flowers attracting plenty of beneficial insects. The flowers produce capsules that turn from pinkish to rich rosy red shades before maturing brown in the fall. Fall color is usually yellowish to purplish, and the winter shrub is quite attractive, with bark on older stems exfoliating into pale tan papery strips. Colorful foliage selections of this widespread native plant have become popular shrubs across commercial and residential landscapes. In the wild, this shrub is usually found on embankments, bluffs, or rises, where it receives more sunlight. Hardy throughout the Midwest.

Ninebark produces white flowers in late spring on a fountain of arching stems.

northern bush-honeysuckle

Diervilla lonicera

rocky woodlands

full sun to part shade

Northern bush-honeysuckle sports nothing spectacular but is a garden-worthy sleeper, more dynamic than many evergreen shrubs. Its flowers reward close inspection, and its foliage is clean and neat, with the new growth of some plants emerging coppery in spring. Fall color is shades of red, from burgundy to scarlet. Plants slowly sucker into a thicket, rarely growing more than 4 feet tall and making a fine low shrub or hedge. Sited closely, they create a sturdy mass planting; northern bush-honeysuckle is a particularly good choice for parking lot islands in the Upper Midwest. It is easy to transplant, thrives in almost any well-drained soil, and is drought tolerant once established. Can take full sun northward but grows best with light shade to afternoon shade. Hardy throughout, thriving even in the heat of the Lower Midwest.

A relative of the garden-mainstay weigela, northern bush-honeysuckle would be just as popular if its glowing yellow flowers were as large.

prairie wild rose

Rosa setigera

upland savannas, woodland edges, hedgerows

full sun to part shade

Prairie wild rose can replace any climbing rose in a traditional landscape. Around the summer solstice clusters of flowers open rich pink but fade to light pink, creating a two-toned effect. The abundant round hips, the most beautiful of any wild rose, are showy in the winter landscape. It makes a large 5-foot-high haystack of arching stems and can climb to 8 feet or more when rambling over other plants or when trained on a trellis. It does not sucker, and its stems do not root where they touch soil. Prairie wild rose thrives in moist, well-drained soil and is more resistant to blackspot than most landscape roses. Prune out dead canes, as you would any climbing rose, to keep the shrub vigorous; if not pruned annually it is best reserved for a natural landscape, where it makes prime wildlife habitat and is a favorite shrub for nesting song-birds—a great replacement for nonnative and invasive multiflora rose.

Prairie wild rose is a spectacular sight when in bloom.

prairie willow
Salix humilis

dry upland glades, prairies

full to part sun

Prairie willow, the most upland of our willows, is criminally underutilized in our landscapes. When pruned to maintain its vigor, it makes a very handsome landscape shrub with foliage that stands out in a garden. The shrub comes off as gray-green with an unusual texture, as the leaves are untoothed, gray-hairy, and with visible leaf veining. The catkins are delightful and the smallest of the spring pussy willows here, and they open to wonderful flowers abuzz with hordes of honeybees and other early pollinating insects. All willows are dioecious: the catkins of male plants are showier, with yellow stamens; the catkins of female plants eventually produce fruits with cottony seeds. Prairie willow easily grows 8–12 feet tall but can be kept smaller by annual rejuvenation after flowering.

Prairie willow's showy male catkins illuminate an early spring day.

pussy willow

Salix discolor

peaty wetlands

full sun to part shade

Pussy willow is one of the most treelike of our Midwest shrub willows and a better landscape plant than the non-native European goat willow (*Salix caprea*), the source of most pussy willows at nurseries, because it doesn't grow nearly so large (usually 10 feet tall, rarely to 20 feet). Pussy willow has lovely smooth, whitened leaf undersides, making it quite showy and adding to its ornamental appeal; it also has the largest early spring catkins of our native willows. It forms an upright crown, usually multistemmed with a thick base, and responds well to being cut back, growing long stems of catkins. It makes a fine, if large, ornamental shrub for traditional landscapes and a good addition to rain gardens and around water gardens. Best in AHS heat zone 6 and cooler.

red-berried elder

Sambucus racemosa var. *pubens*

moist forests

full sun to part shade

This is a charming large shrub for a shady woodland garden or bird-themed garden. The swelling buds, leaf and flower, burst with foliage early in spring and bloom fully by midspring. The puffy flower clusters emerge from red buds and open to creamy white; they have an unusual scent that reminds me of a freshly opened package of rubber bands. The berries ripen to a brilliant red by midsummer; rose-breasted grosbeaks and other birds feast on them, having no trouble spotting the bright berries against all the greens of that season. Red-berried elder does well southward if sheltered from hot summer sun and wind and if sourced from southern populations; in the Lower Midwest, it thrives in shaded, cooler sites on the north or east sides of buildings.

The early spring catkins on male pussy willow plants are adorable.

Red-berried elder produces striking red fruits in midsummer.

red-osier dogwood

Cornus sericea

moist woodlands, wetlands

full sun to part shade

Red-osier dogwood works well in a rain garden and is a fine large shrub (readily growing 8 feet tall) for mass plantings in swales or other wetter sites. It really stands out in a snowy winter landscape with its red stems, some plants more colorful and almost coral red. The flowers are creamy white clusters in late spring. Berries are white on red stems in late summer; they drop, or are eaten by birds, before winter. Fall color can be quite beautiful in shades from yellow and orange to dark red on foliage that receives full sun. This dogwood is stressed under hot and dry conditions. Removing older stems keeps the plant tidier as well as maintains the best red stems—the red color is lost on old wood. Best in AHS heat zone 5 and cooler.

The red stems of red-osier dogwood add color on a dreary winter's day.

Red-osier dogwood berries.

roughleaf dogwood

Cornus drummondii

successional lands, woodland edges

full sun to part shade

No plant in my yard attracts more wildlife than this large, brushy, thicket-forming shrub. I have watched various resident and migrant songbirds come in to snatch its lipid-rich berries—including phoebes, pewees, vireos, and warblers. The white berries, set atop red stems, float like clouds over the shrub in late summer and fall—a phenomenal contrast to the red and burgundy fall foliage. The berries do not last into winter; they wither and drop if not eaten by birds. White-throated sparrows and other ground-feeding birds seek out the seeds of fallen fruit. The creamy white flower clusters bloom in late spring after the plant has leafed out and are visited by masses of pollinators. Leaves have a raspy cat's-tongue surface (hence the common name); their edges curl up, showing a lighter underside. One of the finest screening and hedgerow plants but ornamental enough to serve as a focal specimen, especially if trained into a little tree. Very heat and drought tolerant. Plants are easily propagated by division. Hardy throughout the Midwest.

Roughleaf dogwood fruit attracts songbirds in fall like no other plant.

shrubby cinquefoil

Dasiphora fruticosa

diverse habitats, from dry cliffs to wet fens

full sun to part shade

Shrubby cinquefoil is a compact, rounded shrub, growing to about 3 feet tall. It has finely divided, gray-green foliage and is speckled with yellow flowers, heaviest in early summer, although some flowers are produced into fall. It is suitable for a traditional landscape, where it is often included in low shrub borders. This small shrub is easy to grow in most garden soils given the right light but suffers in rich, heavy clay soils. It does best in the Upper and Eastern Midwest and is more fickle in the western Lower Midwest, as it does not like the heat and humidity of AHS heat zone 7.

silky dogwood

Cornus amomum

upland prairie swales, streamsides, wetland edges, open riparian areas

full sun to part shade

This dogwood is truly a shrub, never a tree, with a multi-stemmed base of greenish to reddish stems. It makes a fine shrub for massing, especially in problematic wet areas, and it works well in rain gardens, as it can take being wet or dry. It readily grows to 8 feet tall. Removing older stems keeps the plant looking tidier. The stems are somewhat ornamental in winter, usually greenish to reddish brown, more colorful on younger stems. Flowers appear in late spring, in clusters of creamy white, followed by unusually colored, bluish berries that ripen in late summer; sometimes the berries are fused blue on white like porcelain. The fruits drop in the fall. Fall color is usually very good from red to burgundy, with yellows and oranges on the shaded leaves. Silky dogwood thrives in full sun to light shade and is tolerant of all but the driest soils. Hardy throughout the Midwest.

Dasiphora fruticosa Dakota Sunspot ('Fargo') stands out with gray-green leaves and yellow flowers.

The bluish fruit of silky dogwood distinguishes it from other native dogwoods.

smooth sumac

Rhus glabra

dry upland woods, grassland edges, roadsides

full sun to part shade

Smooth sumac makes a fine mass planting in well-drained soil on steep embankments or against a woodland or tree planting. The light green flowers, which appear in early to midsummer, are noticeably fragrant. Many insects and woodland butterflies visit the flowers. Female plants produce showy pyramidal clusters of fuzzy reddish fruit which hold through winter. The leaves are dark blue-green above with lighter bluish, luminous undersides that reflect night light; this plant shines in such a situation, near an outdoor seating area or at a front entry, for example. In fall, leaves turn to intense and saturated reds, often with a pinkish overtone. A word to the wise: smooth sumac runs in all directions except toward shade.

Smooth sumac often displays vivid red fall color.

soapweed yucca

Yucca glauca

prairies

full sun

Soapweed yucca, a Great Plains species, grows in well-drained soils on steep loess, rocky, or gravelly substrates. It is a rugged evergreen for a harsh site where many other evergreens would struggle (but it does make a striking companion to shrubby junipers, if they are already present and thriving); the sunny, windswept, rocky end of my driveway is adorned them. The spiky 2-foot-long narrow foliage grows in a striking tuft and is grayish green all year. In early summer, the plant produces a 2- to 3-foot spike of greenish cream pendent flowers that are followed by up-facing seedpod fruits that ripen blackish and remain into winter. The flowers are pollinated by the yucca moth and nothing else, so plants produce no pods where the moth is absent (unless you hand pollinate the flowers). Soapweed yucca is one of the most heat and drought tolerant of all midwestern plants. Hardy throughout the Midwest.

Soapweed yucca's greenish cream flowers are often brushed with rose.

southern arrowwood

Viburnum dentatum

forested slopes, forest edges, woodland openings

full sun to part shade

Southern arrowwood is often a medium-sized shrub in the 5- to 8-foot-tall range, but occasionally can be a large shrub. It makes a perfect informal hedge and does equally well massed at the back of a perennial border or bird garden, offering great wildlife habitat. The foliage is clean and often neatly pleated, turning rich shades from burnt orange to reds and even burgundy tones in fall—sometimes pale yellow to pinkish yellow in light shade. In late spring, malodorous flat clusters of white flowers with a haze of yellow anthers create an overall creamy look; the stinky flowers attract many flies, beetles, and some bees and butterflies. Round fruits ripen in late summer and are a feast for migrant birds including the eastern kingbird, which mainly eats insects before migration; the berries seldom persist after leaf drop. Grows well in almost any moist, well-drained soil but flowers and fruits best in full sun.

Southern arrowwood produces an abundance of blue fruit in late summer.

spicebush

Lindera benzoin

floodplain forests, moist woodlands

full sun to part shade

Its spicy aroma, especially potent in dry twigs and stems, gives this deer-resistant plant its common name. It's a magical addition to a woodland garden or along a stream or pond garden, and birds relish the lipid-rich fruit that female shrubs produce. It hosts two iconic insects—the spicebush swallowtail butterfly and the promethea moth—so it's a must in a butterfly garden. With age and in ideal conditions it becomes a large multistemmed shrub over 15 feet tall. The yellowish tiny flowers are a delight on its bare stems in early spring; the foliage is clean and rich green, folded into leaf tacos that are the daytime shelter of the spicebush swallowtail caterpillar, which ventures out to feed only at night. The berries on female plants are glossy lipstick red in late summer and early fall, followed by a consistent rich yellow fall color that can't be beat. Best grown in at least afternoon shade. Hardy to USDA zone 5b.

The glossy red berries on female plants of spicebush are its finest asset and important fuel for migrating songbirds.

staghorn sumac
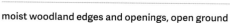

Rhus typhina

moist woodland edges and openings, open ground

full sun to part shade

Staghorn sumac is the largest and most treelike of the running sumacs, reaching 35 feet or more; it makes an excellent edge-of-the-woods or hedgerow planting in large landscapes. Sumac is best known for its flaming fall color, and staghorn sumac's is yellow, orange, or red, often all on the same plant at the same time. Staghorn sumac has the showiest fruit of the sumacs: it's fuzzy with metallic hairs, ripens red in late summer, and lingers through winter; fruits, on female plants, are exceptionally ornamental when adorned with snow. Its young stems, velvety like a stag's horn, are also quite noticeable and usually red-brown in winter. Plants require moist, well-drained soil. Cut back to the ground to rejuvenate. Hardy throughout the Midwest.

Foliage of staghorn sumac creates an interesting herringbone pattern.

swamp wild rose

Rosa palustris

wetlands

full sun to part shade

Swamp wild rose usually grows in a clump, forming a 5- to 6-foot-tall upright vase-shaped shrub with pendent branches. The thorny, arching stems create habitat for nesting songbirds. This native shrub produces typical pink wild rose flowers in midsummer (later than most wild roses) and rose hips in fall that hang on the plant through winter, adding a touch of bright interest to the winter garden. It's a fine suckering shrub for a rain, pondside, or wetland garden. It will grow in good garden soil but prefers a moist to wet soil with a lower pH and may even tolerate standing water.

Swamp wild rose flowers in the wilds of Fernwood, Michigan.

wild hydrangea

Hydrangea arborescens

rocky outcrops and slopes in moist forests

full sun to part shade

Wild hydrangea is best considered a 4- to 5-foot-tall flowering shrub for moist shade, but it will grow in full sun if moisture is available—and the more light, the heavier the flowering. Lightly fragrant, creamy white fertile flowers are surrounded by a few showy sterile flowers, creating what's called a lacecap flower. The flowers appear in midsummer, at a time when few plants are in bloom, and they attract many pollen-collecting insects, especially bumblebees and beetles. Fall color can be a lovely whitish yellow. Fertile flowers produce a flat head of tiny dry seedpod fruits that mature rich brown, sterile flowers age to beige, and together they hold on the plant well through winter. Hardy throughout the Midwest.

The lacecap flowers of wild hydrangea shine in the midsummer sun.

Groundcovers

big-leaf aster

Eurybia macrophylla

Northwoods, moist forests

part to full shade

Big-leaf aster offers a coarser texture than many groundcovers and is suitable for planting in challenging locations—under pines, for example. The large, heart-shaped toothed basal leaves create a 12-inch-thick green carpet from spring through fall, at which season it becomes a calico of various warm-colored autumn shades. Mature plants produce white to light blue flowers in late summer and fall, followed by tufts of fruits (if flowers are cross-pollinated). Flowering stems are formed sparingly and reach 24–30 inches above the foliage, toward the light. This species spreads by underground rhizomes and can be readily divided to create more plants. It prefers well-drained, more acidic soils but will grow in most humus-rich, moist soils; it survives but behaves more like a nonspreading perennial in the heavy clays and heat of western Lower Midwest gardens.

Big-leaf aster forms a dense carpet of heart-shaped leaves by midspring.

cedar sedge

Carex eburnea

dry woodlands, savannas, hill prairies, glades

full sun to full shade

Cedar sedge is so named because it is often found in the wild underneath eastern red cedars, a situation that is the very epitome of dry shade. This widespread sedge is more finely textured (almost hairlike!) than Pennsylvania sedge, and its anthers are more ivory whitish in color, hence its other common name, ivory sedge. Foliage grows to just 8 inches tall. It combines well with other smaller groundcovers and perennials that thrive in dry sites, such as lesser pussytoes, moss phlox, widow's cross sedum, and eastern red columbine. If you are struggling to find a groundcover for dry shade, cedar sedge is a great solution. It's tolerant of light foot traffic and requires virtually no maintenance other than tree seedling and weed removal. Sedges produce seeds that are consumed by many songbirds, and the foliage is host to many moths and a few butterflies, including the dun skipper. Hardy throughout the Midwest.

Cedar sedge spreads slowly from a tufted-looking new planting into a very lawnlike carpet over time.

cream violet

Viola striata

moist woodlands, forests

part to full shade

The short stems and leaves of cream violet, together with its small, black-streaked white flowers, create a refined look in a garden, and both leaves and flowers are edible. The plant reaches only 6–9 inches tall, grows in just about any good, well-drained garden soil, and self-sows abundantly, forming a rather aggressive and solid groundcover in moist shade. It does, however, allow for sturdy woodland perennials to grow through it, so it is a good companion groundcover that "ties the room together," so to speak. Cream violet is often host to caterpillars of the great spangled fritillary. Excellent for shady traditional landscapes.

Both the flowers and leaves of cream violet are edible.

crested iris

Iris cristata

rich wooded slopes, floodplain forests

part to full shade

Another excellent choice for shady traditional landscapes. This plant grows about 6 inches tall and spreads to form a low groundcover; it's especially good for rocky border edges. The spiky short leaf blades add a distinct texture and characterful look to the garden through the entire growing season. This iris is beloved for its blue to rarely white flowers, which are stunningly beautiful but only briefly present, adorning plants in midspring. Crested iris is widely cultivated across our region, thriving in humus-rich, moist but well-drained soils. Propagate by dividing the rhizomes.

The bladelike leaves of crested iris are accompanied by classic blue flowers for a brief time each spring.

foamflower
Tiarella cordifolia

moist forest ravines, swamps, swamp edges

part to full shade

Foamflower blooms in mid to late spring with spires of foamy white flowers that give the plant its name. The foliage is lobed, somewhat maple-shaped, and evergreen, so it looks good in the landscape year-round; the stunningly patterned leaves are especially welcome in winter, when they enliven the woodland garden. This perennial plant grows less than 12 inches tall and makes a memorable shade garden or woodland groundcover in appropriate moist soils or in sustainably irrigated landscapes throughout the Midwest. Although it is not a wetland species, it thrives with constant moisture in well-drained soils in shade. Easily propagated by division.

When in bloom in spring, foamflower creates a tapestry of white flowers, punctuated here by purple creeping phlox.

garden phlox
Phlox paniculata

moist woodlands, woodland edges, savannas, disturbed ground

full sun to part shade

Garden phlox, one of the most popular midwestern garden flowers, produces a large panicle of bright pink-purple (rarely white) flowers atop its leafy stem and blooms for a long period, from late July into September and sometimes later. In fall, the fertile flowers make tiny tan, round fruit capsules that audibly snap open on a dry day, flinging the black seeds a good distance. Plants grow 3–4 feet tall, and they are hummingbird, butterfly, and moth magnets. Self-sows abundantly. Best grown as a groundcover mass with spring ephemerals or other robust herbaceous perennials that can hold their ground against it. New England aster, spotted Joe-Pye weed, tussock sedge, and cream and wild blue violets are good companions. Easy to grow in average garden soil; this long-cultivated species is often an indicator of a forgotten homestead. Avoid its many cultivars: pollinators never (or almost never) visit them, even as they swarm wild-sourced plants nearby.

A mass of wild garden phlox blooms in various shades between pink and purple.

golden groundsel

Packera aurea

low wet woodlands, forested seeps

part sun to full shade

Golden groundsel forms large masses of bright yellow flowers in mid to late spring; the flowers are very rich in nectar and attract many pollinating insects, including butterflies. The plant's nearly evergreen basal foliage remains under 12 inches tall, holds its place through all seasons, and resists deer browse. This is a showy spring groundcover for moisture-rich woodland gardens and shady traditional landscapes; the flower scapes rise 18–30 inches tall in perfect wet, rich-soil conditions. The plant is a fine choice for the lower portions of rain gardens or to infill problematic wet areas in any landscape.

Golden groundsel creates a mass of yellow springtime bloom in a wet woodland garden.

lesser pussytoes

Antennaria neglecta

dry prairies, savannas, woodlands

full sun to part shade

Lesser pussytoes is a great groundcover for exceptionally dry locations in both sun and shade, working well in "hell strips" or underneath an eastern red cedar. In the wild, it inhabits challenging, often eroded spots where little else will compete with its small stature: its basal leaves reach just 3 inches tall, with flower spikes growing up to 8 inches tall. The basal leaves are silvery and finely textured, with a single noticeable vein; they contrast nicely with companion plants. The flowers are tight, silky white clusters, like a little toe. Female flowers produce a tuft of awned fruits that look frothy when ripe, whereas the male flowers quickly disintegrate after flowering. Plants spread by rhizomes into a large mass that may be several feet across. Readily propagated by division.

Lesser pussytoes covers even dry ground.

mistflower

Conoclinium coelestinum

floodplain forests, wooded streamsides

full sun to part shade

Mistflower is sometimes called hardy ageratum, and it does indeed look very much like that popular annual, producing equally beautiful light to medium blue (sometimes white) flowers in late summer. The flowers are very rich in nectar and are visited by many pollinators, including butterflies. Plants grow 24–30 inches tall and spread almost too eagerly by underground rhizomes. Mistflower thrives in almost any soil that is not dry, in full sun to light shade. It's a great plant to control erosion and is on every short list of groundcovers for sunny traditional landscapes, but it is best in natural landscapes, where it must compete with other aggressive species; it should not be planted, uncontained, in a traditional mixed perennial border. Propagate by division.

The abundant blue flowers of mistflower look nearly identical to those of ageratum.

moss phlox

Phlox subulata

savannas, rocky and sandy barrens, disturbed ground

full sun to part shade

Another groundcover suitable for a traditional landscape, especially where a low evergreen carpet is needed in a harsh sunny site. Moss phlox grows about 6 inches tall and spreads by stems that root where they touch the ground, sprawling more than 3 feet across over many years. The plant is smothered in blooms in early to midspring—a veritable mass of color, usually soft blue. Its many selections offer flowers that are variably "eyed" and shaded white, pink, blue, or purplish. Thrives in dry sites.

The orange stamens of moss phlox make a visible "eye" at the center of its flowers.

orange coneflower

Rudbeckia fulgida

moist to wet woodlands, savannas, swamps

full sun

Orange coneflower, a perennial black-eyed Susan, self-sows abundantly and is best left to cover ground with its exuberant flowering masses of summer gold. 'Goldsturm', a selection of its var. *sullivantii* made in the Czech Republic, remains very popular; and several naturally occurring varieties of wild plants make outstanding perennials, suitable for traditional and natural gardens. The fruiting heads of all orange coneflower varieties mature dark brown and hold well through the winter landscape. In the wild, orange coneflower prefers soils that are moist to wet—usually near waterways, edges of marshes, seeps, and fens. Plants grow 2–3 feet tall and make dramatic sweeping masses in larger landscapes. They are often included in traditional perennial borders, and wetland-tolerant varieties make colorful additions to rain gardens and bioswales. Orange coneflower is a favorite host plant for the silvery checkerspot butterfly. Self-sows prolifically, and may also be propagated by division.

The brown-eyed flowers of orange coneflower pair well with garden phlox.

ostrich fern

Matteuccia struthiopteris

floodplain forests, moist forests

part to full shade

Ostrich fern is most beautiful when its fiddleheads emerge in spring; the fresh fronds of vibrant green are widest toward the top and come to an abrupt point. Fully unfurled, plants are vase-shaped and reach 3–4 feet tall. In winter, after the surrounding sterile fronds have died, the stiff, brown plumelike fertile fronds stand around 2 feet tall. This fern requires moist, humus-rich soils and shade; some sun is tolerated in more northern and eastern locations as long as they stay moist. Ostrich fern spreads by ground-hugging rhizomes to create extensive masses; it spreads so quickly and vigorously, it is best used as a tall groundcover in moist, shady sites. Propagate by division.

A May groundcover of ostrich fern fiddleheads will soon be a solid stand of delicate fronds.

Pennsylvania sedge

Carex pensylvanica

savannas, woodlands

part to full shade

If you have never been to a remnant savanna carpeted by a natural, no-mow lawn of Pennsylvania sedge, you are missing out on an experience that proves a lawn need not be nonnative bluegrass. Pennsylvania sedge is a cool-season native that greens up early in spring with fine-textured leaf blades, just like bluegrass, but it never sets a tall inflorescence: its flower is shorter, golden, and torchlike. The blade color is more yellow or golden green and becomes straw-colored in winter. The plant grows 4–6 inches tall and spreads about 6 inches a year, creating a low turflike groundcover for traditional landscapes that never needs mowing. In cultivation, this sedge requires a shady spot with moist to dry, well-drained soil. Like all sedges, it is a wonder for keeping down weeds. It's most easily propagated by division.

Who would want to mow this?

Pennsylvania sedge creates a natural, no-mow lawn in a sand savanna at Sugar River Forest Preserve, Winnebago County, Illinois.

plantain-leaved pussytoes

Antennaria plantaginifolia

upland forest openings, hill prairies, disturbed ground

part sun to part shade

Plantain-leaved pussytoes is very similar to lesser pussytoes, serving just as well as a smothering mass to fill a large space, but it has wider basal leaves (very like those of plantain, hence the common name) that show three noticeable veins. Another difference: plantain-leaved pussytoes grows better with more shade than does lesser pussytoes; its leaves may actually burn if it's in a location that is too sunny, too hot, or too dry. It certainly and willingly covers ground, however, especially in shady traditional landscapes, and is a perfect plant to control areas of soil erosion.

The basal leaves of plantain-leaved pussytoes look remarkably (some would say "uncomfortably") like plantain, a common lawn weed.

river oats

Chasmanthium latifolium

rich woodlands, floodplain forests

full sun to part shade

In the garden, river oats looks lovely for at least six months, as its extremely ornamental seed heads hold well into winter; they may also be cut and dried for bouquets. In the wild, it inhabits rich loamy soils, often on terraces beneath bluffs. This cool-season grass is a host plant to several woodland butterflies, including the northern pearly-eye and little wood-satyr. It does not self-sow much in heavy, poor clay soils, but it does so abundantly in the typically humus-rich, loamy soil of perennial borders. It is much better used in shady traditional landscapes as a tall (2–3 feet) groundcover, where it can seed into a large mass without interfering with prized perennials. With moisture, it will grow in full sun, but it prefers light shade. It languishes in drought-prone soils.

The lovely seed heads of river oats, produced by midsummer, make it one of the most ornamental of woodland grasses.

River oats, pre–fall color.

roundleaf groundsel

Packera obovata

moist to dry upland woods, forests

full sun to part shade

Roundleaf groundsel is fairly similar to golden groundsel but takes better to dry (or at least drier) sites; as such, it is well suited as a tough groundcover for shady traditional landscapes. Its evergreen basal leaves are smaller and more round than those of golden groundsel, and it is more loosely flowered. Its yellow flowers, borne in profusion each spring, are equally rich in nectar, attracting a wide variety of pollinators, and its foliage is the only confirmed host plant for the rare and diminutive northern metalmark butterfly.

The daisy-like flowers of roundleaf groundsel attract a wide variety of pollinators.

Roundleaf groundsel is a great choice for a groundcover in a dry woodland garden setting.

widow's cross sedum

Sedum ternatum

rocky outcrops in woodlands and forests

part to full shade

This sedum makes a low and luscious succulent groundcover, 3–6 inches tall, for a shady or sheltered rock garden or rock wall. The fleshy rounded leaves are rich green, holding in part into winter. The delightful midspring inflorescence is a spreading spike of starry white flowers with stamens that emerge plump and red and mature purplish black. The flowers produce dried brown fruits with four follicles, each follicle containing up to a dozen tiny seeds. In nature, this species is usually found where little else will grow. In a garden setting, it will require protection from rabbits. Plant it in well-drained rocky soil. Thrives in dry sites.

Sedum ternatum 'Larinem Park' in bloom, each inflorescence reminiscent of a giant snowflake.

wild ginger

Asarum canadense

moist woodlands, forests

part to full shade

Wild ginger is a wonderful and unusual groundcover for shady traditional landscapes and a welcome addition to almost any moist woodland garden. Plants grow 6–9 inches tall and spread by rhizomes on or near the surface of well-drained soil. Jug-shaped flowers are produced in spring and hug the ground—opening between the two shiny heart-shaped leaves before they are fully formed. The outermost whorl of the flower, a three-parted calyx, opens to reveal madder red inside. Plants are somewhat variable: some have flowers whose long calyxes open from the beak-shaped flower bud; in others, the calyx lobes are folded inward on the "beak" of the bud. Lower Midwest strains have thicker leaves that are more at home in summer heat. As always, choose regional plants for your garden whenever possible.

The heart-shaped leaves of wild ginger have a taffeta-like sheen.

wild strawberry

Fragaria virginiana

moist to dry prairies, savannas, woodlands, disturbed ground

full sun to part shade

Wild strawberry occurs in all but the hottest and driest parts of North America, and in cultivation, it thrives in almost any well-drained soil. The spring flowers are shockingly white with a yellow center. Fruits are small and red, as ornamental as they are delicious. The three-parted leaves often turn rich red shades in autumn and persist through winter, hugging the ground. This groundcovering species is as aggressive as vinca or English ivy, quickly filling any space. It makes a tremendous stand-alone groundcover in full sun or even dry shade. It is perfect for a natural landscape, where it may run between existing plants, and it should be plugged into established prairie gardens. Wild strawberries are integral plants for edible landscapes and food forests; they have a more intense flavor than the cultivated strawberries hybridized from them. Note: fruit is produced only on female plants.

Wild strawberry produces showy white flowers in midspring.

zigzag goldenrod

Solidago flexicaulis

moist to dry upland forests, woodlands

full sun to part shade

Another great native for covering ground in traditional landscapes. Zigzag goldenrod blooms in midfall, producing wands of classic goldenrod yellow flowers in small tufted clusters at the bases of the stem leaves. It reaches around 2 feet tall, spreads by rhizomes, and makes an ideal mass planting in a shade or natural woodland garden. It also combines well with other woodland wildflowers, blooming at the same time as Short's aster and blue wood aster. Easy to propagate by division.

As its common name implies, zigzag goldenrod's stem is not straight.

Perennials and Vines

alumroot

Heuchera richardsonii

moist to dry upland prairies, savannas, woodlands

full sun to part shade

This handsome perennial can be planted en masse near the edge of a perennial border, in rock gardens, or in semishady woodland gardens. The evergreen leaves are handsome from spring through winter, sometimes with purplish undersides; they seldom reach 12 inches in height. The airy stems of flowers rise 24–30 inches. The flowers themselves reward close inspection; they are light green and asymmetrical, with a longer top side, and sport cute orange protruding stamens—they may not be pink, but hummingbirds appreciate them and nectar from them all the same. Alumroot grows in almost any well-drained soil. It is hands down the hardiest heuchera species, growing on prairies throughout the northern Great Plains.

Alumroot's flowers are subtly beautiful in a light shade of green.

American bittersweet

Celastrus scandens

dry woods, woodland edges, hedgerows

full sun to part shade

American bittersweet is prized for the display of orange-hulled, vermilion fruit on female vines, which brightens up the midwestern landscape as it becomes bare in autumn. The fall color is also consistently an outstanding light yellow. American bittersweet is best grown on a fence or among established shrubs or small trees in a woodland edge. It rarely grows more than 30 feet, and that only when it is trying to reach light. It can add ornamental appeal to a small tree, growing up into the crown and flowering (small, green and little noticed) and fruiting, showing its great color after the host tree drops its leaves. Easy to grow in almost any well-drained soil. Slow to start but extremely drought tolerant once established. Occasionally self-sows.

The fruit of American bittersweet is persistent and holds its color well into winter. Note that both male and female vines must be present for fruit to develop.

anise hyssop

Agastache foeniculum

dry upland forests, prairies, open oak woodlands, savannas

full sun to part shade

Both the flowers and leaves of this popular aromatic perennial herb are edible; they taste just like licorice, and you have only to rub the foliage when passing by to release the anise scent. The violet-blue florets stand out from the more-purply calyxes for a strikingly showy flower that produces a seed head that holds well into winter. The plant is in flower over a long period, from early summer into autumn, and grows 3–4 feet tall. It attracts pollinating and other beneficial insects exceedingly well, making it a premier plant for an insectaries garden; it's used as a companion plant in orchards for this reason. Its fruiting heads attract songbirds, too. Best in more informal landscapes, utilized in an herb border, or included in an edible landscape or food forest. It grows well and has even naturalized throughout our region, self-sowing abundantly in moist, well-drained soils. Hardy throughout the Midwest.

Anise hyssop blooms with butterfly milkweed at White River Gardens in Indianapolis.

aromatic aster

Symphyotrichum oblongifolium

dry, gravelly or rocky prairies, savannas, glades

full sun to part shade

Aromatic aster reaches a height of just 24–30 inches in a full, mounded form, making it a perfect perennial for a traditional flower border or informal hedge, where its late fall bloom is treasured. The foliage is handsome and aromatic, and the silvery lavender-blue flowers are produced prolifically over the entire plant, creating a carpet (or wall, as the case may be) of color; they are exceptionally rich in nectar and pollen and visited in earnest by hordes of pollinators, including the last-of-the-season butterflies. The plant is easy to cultivate in any well-drained garden soil and self-sows abundantly, even to the point of overtaking less-vigorous perennials. You can trim it for tidiness through midsummer, and it will still bloom by fall.

Aromatic aster creates a living wall of purple on the Island Garden at Powell Gardens, Missouri.

big bluestem

Andropogon gerardii

prairies

full sun to part shade

Big bluestem is a midwestern icon, one of the tall grasses of the tallgrass prairie. Elegant tall flowering stems are topped with a three- (or more) parted inflorescence that looks like a turkey's foot—turkey foot is another name for the grass. "Tall" means 3 feet in poor soils in dry years and up to 8 feet in rich soils in moist years. The basal tuft of foliage is 18–36 inches tall, often highlighted with steel blue and sometimes wine purple. Fall color is variable but always warm tones: from gold and orange-russet to reddish. Big bluestem is most suitable to natural landscapes and prairie gardens. It grows largest in full sun and deep rich soils but does fine in light shade, albeit with weaker flowering, and is shorter in poorer, drier soils. Readily self-sows into tall, dense masses; it is best grown with other plants to give it some competition, which will also reduce seedlings. Hardy throughout the Midwest.

The tall culms of big bluestem display a blend of colors in early fall.

black-eyed Susan

Rudbeckia hirta

prairies, meadows, roadsides

full sun to part shade

Black-eyed Susans, a classic wildflower beloved by all, are short-lived perennials, at best. The blooms, glowing golden yellow ray flowers surrounding the dark brown disc flowers, appear in midsummer and occasionally into fall, and the dried seed heads remain attractive in the winter garden. Plants grow 18 inches to rarely 3 feet tall. They make a perfect cover crop when establishing a prairie garden, suppressing weeds and creating a quick splash of bloom, but diminishing in cover as other longer-lived plants take hold. Dead-heading will extend the bloom season and lengthen the life of the plant, but by removing spent flowers, you also ruin the winter interest of the plant and rob wildlife of its seeds. Black-eyed Susans are best in natural landscapes, where they are allowed to self-sow, or treated as an annual in flowerbeds; they also make nice container subjects. Plants are tolerant of a wide range of soils from wet to dry; they will grow in part shade but are at their best in full sun.

Black-eyed Susan adds to the natural beauty of a prairie garden in Pettis County, Missouri.

bloodroot

Sanguinaria canadensis

moist upland forests

part to full shade

Bloodroot is a quintessential wildflower for a woodland or shade garden. The early spring flowers are quite showy—pristine white petals encircling a bunch of eggyolk yellow stamens surrounding a central green pistil. The flower buds are often tinged pink in cool weather and are equally beautiful. The leaves are exquisitely shaped, with deep undulating lobes forming a distinctive shieldlike form around the flower and developing fruit. Bloodroot provides copious pollen for spring-active bees. It prefers humus-rich, loamy soils. The fleshy root can be divided after the plant goes dormant.

The luminous white flowers of bloodroot are very short-lived, opening only on sunny days in early spring.

blue wild indigo

Baptisia australis

moist to dry upland prairies, savannas

full sun to part shade

Blue wild indigo is the most popular of the wild indigos in cultivation and well represented in perennial gardens of traditional landscapes. In late spring, the stunningly beautiful indigo-blue flowers appear in spikes above the foliage. The foliage is handsome and tidy, turning an interesting black in the fall. The pea pods form green and ripen to black in autumn, adorning the plant through winter. Most plants sold at typical nurseries are the robust eastern (var. *australis*) form, which grows quite large, 3–4 feet tall and wide. Plants native west of the Mississippi and purchased at native plant nurseries are var. *minor* (sometimes called dwarf blue wild indigo), which makes a much smaller and tidier plant, only 18–24 inches tall. Obviously, a gardener needs to know which form they have and use it appropriately, whether in a traditional perennial border, foundation planting, or prairie garden. In nature, blue wild indigos often grow in rocky soil; in cultivation, they do well in most well-drained soils.

Blue wild indigo is a shrublike perennial suitable for a foundation planting.

blue wood aster

Symphyotrichum cordifolium

moist upland forests, woodlands

full sun to part shade

Blue wood aster's basal leaves, the inspiration for its scientific epithet, are heart-shaped (cordate); stem leaves are toothed and ovate. The individual daisylike flowers are small, but together they form lovely full flower heads in fall. Plants grow 2–3 feet tall and are integral to a woodland or natural shade garden—looking best in billowing masses or mixed with other fall-blooming asters, goldenrods, and woodland grasses. The late-season flowers of all woodland asters, like the flowers of prairie asters, are rich in nectar for diverse pollinators, and their seeds are tufted with a pappus and sought by many songbirds and small mammals. Blue wood aster self-sows abundantly in rich soils.

Blue wood aster produces delightful whitish blue flowers in abundance each fall.

bottlebrush grass

Elymus hystrix

savannas, woodlands

full sun to part shade

This cool-season grass is well named: its inflorescences look like stiff, open bottlebrushes that dry and hold well into winter. The basal leaf blades green up early and produce inflorescences by midsummer. Flowering can be interesting on close inspection when the anthers are present; the resulting fruiting heads dry blond-tan and look extra beautiful with a dark backdrop or when backlit by sunshine. Bottlebrush grass is only one of our native woodland wild rye grasses. Plants grow 30–40 inches tall and can form attractive mass plantings in natural landscapes. They provide a good structure for companion wildflower plantings in shade and woodland gardens, as their foliage and seed heads persist well into winter, creating interest in that quiet season. Bottlebrush grass is easy to grow in most rich soils; it forms clumps that may be divided.

The flower and seed heads of bottlebrush grass clearly depict how the plant got its common name.

bottle gentian
Gentiana andrewsii

moist to wet prairies, savannas, sedge meadows, fens

full sun to part shade

This is probably the easiest gentian to cultivate in rich, moist soils—any good garden soil is just fine. And the flowers are nothing short of a heavenly royal blue, a memorable experience to all who see them, aging purplish or tinted wine red. They bloom at the end of the growing season, usually in September and October, so are a welcome last floral hurrah in any garden. The rich green leaves turn gold with ruddy highlights after plants flower. Bottle gentian is best grown with other plants in a perennial border or natural garden; good companion plants include tussock sedge, soft rush, and Shreve's blueflag or zigzag irises. A patient wait near this plant will reveal large bumblebees as its pollinators—strong enough to open its twisted "closed" and fringed top, they crawl inside the flower. Bottle gentian can grow as tall as 3 feet but is usually lower, as stems splay outward when they mature. Sturdiest in full sun, more decumbent in light shade.

Bottle gentian, growing through vinca.

Bradbury bergamot

Monarda bradburiana

moist to dry upland woods, savannas

full sun to part shade

The delicately showy flowers of Bradbury bergamot are tinted light lilac-white with darker purple spots; they are produced in a ring around a central disk. The ornamental fruiting head that follows holds well into winter. The foliage is clean and resistant to mildew; it turns rich shades of purplish and red in fall. The plant grows about 2 feet tall and is suitable for a traditional perennial border, mass planting, or interspersed in a woodland garden. It attracts many pollinators and is therefore integral to insectaries and butterfly gardens, particularly so as it flowers in late spring, between abundant spring and midsummer blooms. This species may be grown in any well-drained garden soil. Easy to propagate by division.

The unusual flowering heads of Bradbury bergamot are attractive to bees and butterflies.

brown-eyed Susan

Rudbeckia triloba

wet prairies, streamsides, open low woodlands

full sun

Brown-eyed Susans are somewhat like mini black-eyed Susans—the flowers are one-fourth the size but produced in abundance, forming a dome of brown and gold over the plant. The winter fruit seed heads are dark brown but have a warm orange inner glow to them like no other plant. This mainly biennial species is best in a natural garden, where its spontaneous nature can be celebrated. Brown-eyed Susan grows well in any rich, moist to wet soil. It self-sows abundantly in bare soil, in moist cracks on the edges of walks, in the low sections of rain gardens, or wetland swales.

Self-sown brown-eyed Susan enlivens a moist space between a concrete walk and a rock wall.

bugbane

Cimicifuga racemosa

moist woodlands

full sun to full shade

No plant provides more drama in the midsummer perennial border, edge of a woodland, or woodland garden than this plant. Bugbane can tower 4–7 feet tall under ideal growing conditions. It is a pollen source for many insects and is the sole host plant for the Appalachian blue butterfly, whose caterpillars feed on its flowers and developing fruits. The magnificent spires of perfectly rounded buds open from the bottom up into fringed, milky white flowers—always a standout in the mid- to late-summer woodland garden, when few other plants are blooming. The foliage is attractive all growing season and turns yellow shades in the fall. Bugbane is best in part shade, but it will grow in full sun under continually moist conditions.

Tall spires of white flowers make bugbane one of the most spectacular of all native wildflowers.

Bush's poppy-mallow

Callirhoe bushii

prairies, woodlands, glades

full sun to part shade

Poppy-mallows are often called winecups, for the color and form of their up-facing flowers, which have five overlapping petals. The classic bright fuchsia-pink flowers of this, the largest of the poppy-mallows, are produced in abundance through midsummer, attracting bees and butterflies, including the common checkered skipper. Bush's poppy-mallow is an Ozark Highland endemic—and yet makes a good garden subject. It is tall, growing 18–30 inches, and can flop without adjacent plants as support. It demands well-drained garden soil. Self-sows in ideal garden conditions, so it is best in a natural landscape, where it makes a vibrant display. The plant is also an obvious choice for a butterfly garden.

Bush's poppy-mallow forms an upright bushy perennial of stunning fuchsia flowers at Powell Gardens, Missouri.

butterfly milkweed

Asclepias tuberosa

moist to dry prairies, savannas, glades, open ground

full sun

Is there any wildflower more energizing, stimulating the mind with its warm colors? Butterfly milkweed produces the most vibrant orange (occasionally vermilion red or even golden yellow) flowers of any native plant. They occur in early to midsummer with an occasional flower later in summer. The plant is leafier than most milkweeds. Leaves are narrow, strappy, and fine-textured. Narrow pod-shaped fruits hold well into winter, crowning the stems. Unlike most milkweeds, which are short-lived perennials, butterfly milkweed may live for decades. The activity of all its pollinators adds to its buzz as a masterpiece of art and science. This milkweed is an ideal perennial for a traditional perennial border and grows 24–30 inches tall. It thrives in harsh sites as well, making an excellent plant in a rock garden or other hot, sunny location with good drainage. Butterfly milkweed flourishes in average to well-drained soil that may be rocky, gravelly, or sandy. Some strains even grow in pure clay, but most demand fast-draining soils.

A vibrant mass of butterfly milkweed thrives at the University of Michigan's Matthaei Botanical Gardens.

cardinal flower

Lobelia cardinalis

moist to wet floodplains

full sun to part shade

I'm not sure any flower is redder than this. The long flower spikes bloom from the bottom up for six weeks in late summer and early fall, during migration of hummingbirds. A profile of this exquisite flower perfectly fits the head of ruby-throated hummingbirds, its primary pollinator, and a few butterflies with long proboscises, such as the spicebush swallowtail and cloudless sulphur, visit to nectar on the flowers. Cardinal flower grows 3–5 feet tall, and its fruiting heads add interest to the landscape in late fall. It's best in natural gardens along a stream or river; plants self-sow in bare, moist soils. It's often planted in rain gardens and perennial borders, and it's a quintessential plant for a hummingbird garden. Separate the basal offshoots of this short-lived perennial each May, and plant them singly to keep a planting thriving indefinitely. Do not mulch except as a protective covering in winter.

Foreground or background, cardinal flower demands attention.

White pollen-covered stigmas above brilliant red petals define cardinal flower. Hummingbirds develop white racing stripes of pollen on the crown of their heads while it is in bloom.

Christmas fern

Polystichum acrostichoides

moist forests

part to full shade

The dark green fronds of Christmas fern are evergreen. The fiddleheads unfurl exquisitely in spring, hold upright all summer, then lie flat through the winter. The plant reaches about 2 feet tall and is a premier choice for a woodland garden, mass planting, or traditional perennial border in shade, offering ornamental interest in all seasons. Although in the wild it prefers more acidic soils, Christmas fern can be cultivated in almost any moist, well-drained garden soil, so long as it is shaded. Do give it protection from hot summer winds.

The fully furled fronds of Christmas fern.

The newly emerged fiddleheads of Christmas fern rise above last season's evergreen fronds.

cinnamon fern

Osmunda cinnamomea

wet forests

part to full shade

Cinnamon fern makes a magnificent vase-shaped foliage perennial, 3 feet tall. The unfurling fiddleheads are cloaked in rusty woolly hairs that are memorably showy and give this plant its names. In a mature plant, the fertile fronds in the center are like flames of orange-brown in late spring to early summer, surrounded by arching green sterile fronds. The fertile fronds disintegrate by late summer. Give this fern what it prefers in the wild: shade and at least seasonally wet, sandy or other acidic-based, organic or humus-rich soils. It's best in waterside gardens or sites with extra moisture, including containers; in woodland gardens, it usually languishes without extra moisture or regular irrigation. The rhizomes of mature plants may be divided.

The orange-brown fertile fronds standing at the center of arching green sterile fronds identify this as cinnamon fern.

common milkweed

Asclepias syriaca

prairies, savannas, disturbed open ground

full sun to part shade

All milkweeds are premier insectaries plants that attract hordes of butterflies and other pollinators; they are the sole host plant for the monarch. In common milkweed, the 4-inch-wide spheres of flowers are distinctly and pleasantly fragrant. Each flower is bicolored—light pink with rosy pink petals—and individual flowers age tarnished orange-pink. The flowers occur where the leaves meet the stem, on the upper portion of the plant. Leaves are broad and flat, displaying a coarse texture. The fall seedpod fruits are warty and fat, bursting with fluffy seeds, and remain though the winter. Common milkweed is best in natural landscapes, where it grows around 3 feet tall and can be allowed to run underground into a thicket of plants. In good soils without competition, plants may grow 5 or 6 feet tall. Can be aggressive once established, but it's easy to pull unwanted spears of new plants, which won't return in that location.

The fragrant flowers of common milkweed look like pink popcorn balls.

compass plant
Silphium laciniatum

moist to dry prairies

full sun to part shade

Can you imagine crossing a flat prairie that stretches as far as the eye can see, and it's a cloudy day and you need to know your direction? Compass plant, with its leaves that are generally aligned north to south, will guide your way. The leaves of this large perennial reach upward around 3 feet tall and often develop yellow fall color; flower stalks top out at 5–8 feet tall. In the landscape, compass plant is best reserved as a fine sentinel for the back of a perennial border. Its foliage and form make it a good gateway plant— paired on either side of a walk or driveway between garden spaces, and as a classic and widespread prairie plant, it's obviously an important component of prairie gardens. Compass plant grows well in almost any well-drained soil in full sun. If planted in too much shade, its flower stalk will not be sturdy and upright.

The large, intricately divided basal leaves of compass plant make it a dramatic foliage plant in the home landscape.

cream wild indigo

Baptisia bracteata

moist to dry upland prairies, savannas

full sun to part shade

Cream wild indigo is the first of our native wild indigo species to flower in midspring, attracting a large number of native bees. The foliage is handsome all season, and the pea pods, like the flower clusters, form low, disguised in the foliage of companion prairie plants. This wild indigo makes a fine edging perennial in a traditional perennial border as long as companion plants, such as sideoats grama, little bluestem, and prairie dropseed, are used. It shows nicely with shorter perennials and grasses in rock gardens, and it's a necessity for adding spring interest in a prairie garden. Best established as a seedling plug. Cream wild indigo can be fickle but in the end will survive in most well-drained garden soils (sandy, gravelly, or black organic).

The gorgeous creamy yellow flower clusters of cream wild indigo splay outward from a low dome of gray-green foliage.

Culver's root

Veronicastrum virginicum

moist to wet prairies, savannas, woodlands

full sun to part shade

Culver's root makes a striking back-of-the-border perennial, growing 4–6 feet tall. The narrowly pyramidal, striking spires of white flowers complement the protruding salmon-colored stamens and a corresponding cloud of pollinators busy climbing the flower towers. The foliage is whorled and evenly spaced along the stem, creating a very architectural look. The seed heads are also handsome and hold well into the winter landscape. It's a long-lived perennial that stays put, so is suitable for a traditional landscape perennial border. It is a great addition to a natural landscape, especially in woodland gardens, where its midsummer bloom is welcome. Culver's root thrives in average to rich garden soils. Rarely self-sows in a garden.

A honeybee visits the central spire of a Culver's root inflorescence.

cup plant
Silphium perfoliatum

moist meadows, woodland edges, open riparian areas

full sun to part shade

The form of cup plant is very architectural, with paired leaves marching synchronously up sturdy squar-ish stems. Its perfoliate leaves form a V-shaped cup at the stem that collects rainwater—and dew during a drought, when songbirds heavily utilize it as a water source. The deep yellow flowers, like 3-inch-wide sun-flowers, are produced in clusters above the foliage; they are rich in nectar and pollen and attract a diverse group of pollinators. Many songbirds also seek the seed fruits in autumn, more so than sunflowers. This striking plant grows 5–8 feet tall, and though it blackens after a freeze, it remains an interesting presence into winter. It can be carefully maintained as a mass in a bed but is best in a natural landscape, where other plants will compete with it. In rich garden soils without competing vegetation, cup plant grows to gargan-tuan proportions and self-sows with abandon. It prefers full sun but will flower well in part shade.

A massive clump of blooming cup plant commands attention in a traditional flower border in Chicago's Lincoln Park neighborhood.

dotted horsemint

Monarda punctata

sand prairies, sand savannas

full sun to part shade

The flowers of dotted horsemint, arranged in tiered whorls along the top of the stem, attract an amazing array of pollinators. The pointed leafy bracts whorled between these layers of flowers are often whitish or silvery and tinged with pink—an extraordinary composition that shows well even after the flowers have gone to seed. Plants are about 2 feet tall. Dotted horsemint is valued as a long-blooming if short-lived perennial suitable for a container or flower border, and it is one of the finest choices for an insectaries garden, drawing in as it does so many beneficial/predatory insects. Requires well-drained soils, thriving and self-sowing in almost pure sand. Best treated as an annual in normal garden soils.

Pink-blushed bracts separate dotted horsemint's whorls of purple-spotted, parchment-colored flowers.

Dutchman's breeches

Dicentra cucullaria

moist forests over limestone, rocky woodlands

part to full shade

The highly divided fernlike foliage of Dutchman's breeches is beautiful from emergence into late spring. The flowers are pendent, inflated, and translucent, which adds to their sparkling white character. Plants are about 12 inches in height. This native perennial is a classic addition to shade or woodland rock gardens, woodland slopes, or shaded raised beds with improved drainage. Dutchman's breeches needs humus-rich, well-drained soil. It goes dormant by early summer, after which its dormant tuberous roots can be divided.

The luminous white flowers of Dutchman's breeches are well named as they look like upside-down pantaloons.

eastern red columbine

Aquilegia canadensis

rocky outcrops, rocky or sandy woodlands, savannas

full sun to part shade

The 3-foot-tall candelabra of dangling scarlet flowers blooms in late spring over several weeks; midsummer's up-facing fruiting capsules disperse black, pepperlike seeds and quickly disintegrate. The basal tuft of evergreen leaves, less than 12 inches in height, are often marked by the cursive stylings of a leaf-mining micro moth whose caterpillar is small enough to feed inside the thin leaf. Awe-inspiring! Plants are pollinated by ruby-throated hummingbirds and occasionally the spicebush swallowtail and other butterflies with long proboscises; children and stealing bees can cut the nectary for its sweet treat, too. Eastern red columbine thrives in dry sites and persists in a garden only where the soil has the extra drainage of rock, gravel, or sand. Best used in a rock garden, raised bed, rock wall, or in between stepping stones or other stone or concrete work, where it readily self-sows. The plant is also a great choice for a container garden.

The very showy flowers of eastern red columbine provide a magnificent display each spring.

false dragonhead

Physostegia virginiana

moist to wet prairies, open floodplain forests, wetland edges

full sun to part shade

The tubular flowers, arranged on a spike at the top of a stem, are very showy when in bloom in late summer; they may be white to soft pink or pale lavender and are pollinated by insects with long proboscises, including sphinx moths. I know of no other plant that is so obedient—you can move the flowers side to side, and they stay where you put them. But false dragonhead becomes aggressive in gardens without competing plants, running by underground rhizomes to form an extensive thicket in moist, rich soils, and is therefore a better choice for natural gardens than for traditional gardens. It readily grows 3–4 feet tall in good garden soil and even wet soils. Easiest to propagate by dividing a clump.

False dragonhead produces stunning towers of flowers.

false Solomon's seal

Maianthemum racemosum

moist forests, woodlands, woodland edges

part shade

The British Royal Horticultural Society has given this plant an Award of Garden Merit, and yet—even though it far outshines popular perennials like astilbe—false Solomon's seal remains sadly underused in traditional landscapes in its North American homeland. The plumes of frothy, creamy white flowers are a welcome sight during their early summer bloom, a strong contrast to the prevailing greens of that season. The fruits are just as showy and for a long period, turning bronzy gold with reddish spangles by midsummer and ripening to a ruby red by fall, often adorning a plant in golden fall color. False Solomon's seal makes a 24-inch-tall clump, spreading slowly by rhizomes in a shady perennial border or in a natural woodland garden and often forming large masses on the edge of woods. Easy to grow and easily divided.

foxglove penstemon

Penstemon digitalis

prairies, savannas, open ground

full sun to part shade

This penstemon is suitable for a traditional perennial border: it grows about 30 inches tall and stays in a clump. The showy white flowers are shaped like foxgloves on upright stems above the mainly basal foliage; they bloom in early summer—more welcome flowers in the greens of June. The seedpod fruits often turn reddish in late summer, dry brown in fall, and hold well into winter. Foxglove penstemon should be considered for an evening garden, where its white flowers glow and attract pollinating sphinx moths. It is also a fitting plant for a natural landscape, in the company of open trees, or prairie garden. It attracts many species of pollinators from hummingbirds to bees, including one mason bee that is a penstemon specialist. Foxglove penstemon readily grows in well-drained garden soil.

False Solomon's seal produces plumes of creamy white flowers in early summer.

The white flowers of foxglove penstemon sparkle at Powell Gardens, Missouri.

goatsbeard

Aruncus dioicus

moist forests and ravines

full sun to part shade

The tiny creamy white flowers of goatsbeard are produced in frothy abundance on plumelike panicles that tower over the attractive compound leaves. The flowers on male plants are a tad showier, with their stamens, but disintegrate after bloom. The flowers on female plants produce seed capsule fruits that ripen brown and hold into winter, adding interest to the plant. The foliage reliably turns yellow in the fall. Goatsbeard grows into a large shrublike perennial 3–4 feet tall and even wider. It is suitable for a traditional perennial border, edge of a woodland, or replacement for foundation shrub. It attracts a wide array of pollinators and is the sole host plant for the rare dusky azure butterfly. Plants do best in moist, well-drained soils.

When in flower, goatsbeard illuminates the deep June greens of this woodland edge.

golden alexanders

Zizia aurea

open upland woods, savannas, prairies

full sun to part shade

The tiny flowers of this premier late-spring pollinator plant are held in dense umbels that "read" as flat lenses of intense yellow in the garden. The umbels are full of fruits by late summer, and the lush deep green foliage turns orange and red shades in the fall. Plants reach 2–3 feet tall; they are caterpillar host plants for the black swallowtail and the rare endemic Ozark swallowtail. Golden alexanders is valued for its early bloom in prairie gardens, where intense competition from other plants helps control it. In traditional landscapes, site it in poorer soils among established plants; it makes a beautiful companion to eastern red columbine in rocky sites. Easy to grow in just about any well-drained soil. It self-sows to the point of being a nuisance in rich soils without competing plants. Hardy throughout the Midwest.

The yellow inflorescence of golden alexanders is reminiscent of Queen Anne's lace, a familiar nonnative.

Goldie's fern

Dryopteris goldiana

moist forests, woodlands

part to full shade

Goldie's fern is our most spectacular wood fern, growing as much as 4 feet tall in the right conditions. Its large, somewhat triangular fronds adorn scaly straw-colored stalks, 12–16 inches long. It and all wood ferns take readily to moist, well-drained soil in shady gardens, spreading slowly by rhizomes into multicrowned plants that can be divided. Wood ferns make beautiful additions to traditional shade and woodland gardens, where they can be planted en masse or integrated with other spring ephemerals or woodland plants. Their doubly pinnately compound fronds add a very fine texture to the garden; they are more leathery than the fronds of other ferns, remaining evergreen but lying flat in the winter.

Magnificent Goldie's fern stands tall in front of a mass of maidenhair fern.

grape creeper
Parthenocissus inserta

open rocky forests, forest edges, rocky outcrops

full sun to full shade

Grape creeper is a nearly identical first cousin to Virginia creeper; but it does not grow as large as Virginia creeper, and it is more apt to creep along the ground. This woody vine climbs by grapelike tendrils that wrap around or cling to its support but more often it sprawls over the ground, in which case its foliage may be slightly larger than it is when growing upward, with a more abrupt and toothed end to the leaf. Another underutilized native vine, perfect for a traditional landscape.

Grape creeper as seen wild at the Minnesota Zoo.

gray goldenrod
Solidago nemoralis

prairies, dry open ground, roadsides

full sun to part shade

Gray goldenrod has the classic shape of a goldenrod inflorescence: a plume whose leader arches sideways. The flower is typical golden yellow, and the leaves are a nicely contrasting gray-green, turning orange to red in the fall. In nature, this native perennial is found in very poor, open soils that are often sandy, gravelly, or rocky, but it grows in nearly any well-drained soil, becoming almost unrecognizably large in rich, good soil, to 3 feet tall and more. It is does well in rock gardens and is a perfect solution for hot, dry "hell strips" and other challenging sites (although it is usually less than 2 feet tall in such spots). Gray goldenrod stays in a clump and doesn't overly self-sow.

Gray goldenrod flowers punctuate shorter prairie grasses.

Gray's sedge
Carex grayi

floodplain forests, woodlands

full sun to part shade

Woodland sedges are some of the most underutilized plants of our midwestern flora. Whether purchased from a native plant nursery or inherited as wild plants or as self-sown "volunteers," they should be treasured. In the garden, you can move them into bed edges or between stepping stones, or plant them in sweeping masses. They are cool-season plants, growing early like cool-season grasses. They produce little-noticed flowers (a few are more conspicuous) in spring and are fruiting by late spring, with their fruits usually gone by midsummer. Gray's sedge grows about 2 feet tall with an equal spread and produces distinctive spiky rounded fruits.

The spiky rounded fruits of Gray's sedge make it easy to identify.

great blue lobelia

Lobelia siphilitica

openings in floodplain forests, moist to wet prairies
and meadows

full sun to part shade

This lobelia produces tall showy spires of light to rich blue flowers in late summer, a bloom season that coincides with that of cardinal flower, but great blue lobelia is pollinated by bees, mainly bumblebees. Plants grow about 3 feet tall and are tolerant of a wide range of soils, as long as they are not dry. Like cardinal flower, this rather short-lived perennial needs to be divided or allowed to self-sow to persist. This adaptation makes great blue lobelia best suited to a natural garden—or a close-to-home perennial bed where you can easily keep an eye on it and give it extra attention.

Great blue lobelia blooms on a roadside near Decorah, Iowa.

Indiangrass
Sorghastrum nutans

moist to dry upland prairies

full sun

This warm-season grass is an important component of the tallgrass prairie, but you can bring it home: Indiangrass grows exceedingly well in average garden soil. In late summer and early fall, a golden yellowish plume of flowers adorned with showy yellow stamens appears atop the stem. The fruiting heads age from coppery to tawny, and these hairy awn-tipped seed fruits are stunning when backlit. Many songbirds also seek the seed fruits in autumn. Plants reach 4–6 feet tall, occasionally taller. Indiangrass makes a marvelous nontraditional mass planting with big bluestem and switchgrass, and of course is an integral grass for a prairie garden, but it should be present in low quantities so it doesn't overtake a planting. Self-sows abundantly.

A stand of Indiangrass looks coppery in early autumn.

interrupted fern
Osmunda claytoniana

moist forests and clearings

part to full shade

Interrupted fern arises from a slowly creeping, ground-hugging rhizome. The fiddleheads unfurl earlier than those of most ferns, revealing sterile leaflets interrupted about two-thirds up the frond's stalk by fertile leaflets composed entirely of clusters of spores. Above the fertile leaflets, at the end of the leaf stalk, there are again sterile leaflets. The fertile leaflets start dark green but become brown with spore cases in late summer, a sharp contrast to the green of the sterile leaflets above and below them on the stalk. In the garden it prefers moist, well-drained soil; full shade is a must in drier parts of the Midwest. This large fern grows 3 feet tall or more and creates a fine mass planting in woodland gardens; in rich soils it can become huge, perhaps the Midwest's largest fern, to 6 feet tall. It is also a striking container plant. To propagate, simply divide growing points off the rhizome.

A magnificent mass of interrupted fern thrives at the Eloise Butler Wildflower Garden in Minneapolis.

Jack-in-the-pulpit

Arisaema triphyllum

all but the driest woodlands

part to full shade

Jack-in-the-pulpit is beloved for its inflorescence: the "pulpit" is a striated spathe that shelters "Jack," the flower's spadix. The spathe may be green or purplish but is always striped. No one can resist lifting up the pointed hood of the flower to see Jack inside. As the spathe withers, the developing fruit looks like a drumstick of fleshy green berries that mature to a glossy lipstick red. Birds and small mammals relish the ripe berries. The stems are often flecked with purple or dark green, and the lush three-parted leaves hold into late summer, depending on available moisture and rainfall. The plant grows 1–3 feet tall and is an integral addition to a shady perennial border, shade garden, or natural woodland garden, where it will thrive in humus-rich, well-drained soils.

The striated spathes of Jack-in-the-pulpit are distinctive.

Kentucky wisteria

Wisteria frutescens

floodplain forests

full sun

Fragrant, pendent strands of purple flowers draping leafless springtime vines are what come to mind when one mentions wisteria. Well, that would be the Asian wisterias, which are massive vines that can quickly engulf anything they are planted on, including mature shade trees. Our native wisteria produces similar (though unscented) flowers in late spring, after the leaves emerge, on a vine that never becomes problematic. Lavender-blue (rarely white) flowers are borne in 12-inch-long racemes; the fruit is a hanging pea pod that matures to a polished mahogany and can persist through winter, adding interest. Plants are host to the silver-spotted skipper butterfly, whose caterpillar wraps the pinnately compound foliage around itself as a shelter for feeding and pupating. Kentucky wisteria is a beautiful subject for a pergola, arbor, porch, or other structure suitable for a vine. It is easy to cultivate in any good garden soil, growing 12–15 feet, occasionally larger; it can climb up larger trees but will not overtake them. Self-sows prolifically in disturbed soil. Hardy throughout the Midwest.

This wild-collected Kentucky wisteria shows exceptionally long racemes of flowers.

lady fern
Athyrium filix-femina

moist forests

part to full shade

Thin wiry stalks and lobed subleaflets contribute to the fine, lacy effect of lady fern's fronds—probably the finest texture of any substantial woodland garden plant. This is a divine fern for any traditional shade garden or natural woodland planting. It grows 24–30 inches tall and spreads slowly by rhizomes, making a fine mass planting or knitting itself as a companion into spring ephemerals and other woodland plants. Lady fern is our easiest-to-grow fern in moist, well-drained soil, given at least afternoon shade. Propagate by division.

Newly emerged lady fern takes its place among the acid greens of spring.

lanceleaf coreopsis

Coreopsis lanceolata

sand prairies, sand savannas

full sun to part shade

Lanceleaf coreopsis makes a tidy perennial, usually no more than 2 feet tall when in bloom. The 2- to 3-inch flowers are brilliant and saturated golden yellow like no other; they are carried in a dome over the foliage in early summer, but the show is brief, lasting only about two weeks. The basal leaves are about 8 inches long and remain lush through the season. Fruiting heads turn brownish black when ripe and are sought by songbirds. Unlike many plants from sandy native habitats, lanceleaf coreopsis is easy to cultivate in almost any well-drained garden soil. It self-sows into masses, but only lightly, so is suitable for a traditional garden, and it is a phenomenal plant for hot, dry "hell strips" and other sandy or rocky sites, requiring no extra irrigation to survive in such challenging settings. Hardy throughout the Midwest.

A sweep of blooming lanceleaf coreopsis is visited by great spangled fritillaries.

large-flowered bellwort
Uvularia grandiflora

moist forests, woodlands

part to full shade

This quintessential native for the woodland garden blooms in spring and becomes a 2-foot-tall foliage plant that holds through the growing season (with adequate rainfall). The plants emerge upward but bend over as they grow, a botanical ballet producing nodding, light to golden yellow flowers, themselves shaped like a drooping pinwheel. The emerging foliage is bluish or purplish but matures true green, holds clean through the summer, and turns golden in fall or if stressed by summer drought (in the wild, plants go dormant during summer droughts). Ants collect the ripe seeds for food (as with many spring-flowering woodland ephemerals, they are coated in a fatty elaiosome), inadvertently transporting and planting the seed. Ideally, give large-flowered bellwort (aka merrybells) limestone-based, well-drained, humus-rich, loamy soils. Large clumps are easily divided as the plants go dormant in late summer or fall.

Look closely and you will see a tiny green planthopper on the yellow sepal of this large-flowered bellwort.

large-flowered penstemon

Penstemon grandiflorus

dry prairies

full sun

Large-flowered penstemon blooms in early summer, with flowers in clear shades from lavender and pink to white. The paired leaves are smooth and blue-gray-green, a color that contrasts nicely with other plants in the landscape; they look like open clamshells along the upright stem. The seedpod fruits hold well into winter, serving songbirds, and bumblebees pollinate the flowers. Large-flowered penstemon is a 2- to 3-foot-tall, short-lived perennial for a rock garden or above a wall; the plant is also a great choice for a container garden. It needs exceedingly well-drained garden soils to thrive and is best suited to natural gardens with appropriate sandy, loess, or gravelly settings, where it can self-sow and persist.

Large-flowered penstemon is variable, with both white and lilac flowers even within a small stand.

large-flowered trillium

Trillium grandiflorum

moist forests, woodlands

part to full shade

The outward-facing bloom of this beloved woodland wildflower sits on a short pedicel and lasts a long time. It is the showiest flower of our trilliums, with milky white petals and an eye of yellow stamens in midspring; flowers turn rosy pink as they age. Some plants produce flowers with stacked or fully double petals; double-flowering trilliums are highly prized by shade gardeners, but such flowers are sterile, producing no pollen or fruits. Plants reach 12–15 inches tall and are readily cultivated in woodland, shade, or wildflower gardens throughout the Midwest. All trilliums may be propagated by dividing their rhizomes; this is best done as the plant is going dormant in late summer or fall.

The white flowers of large-flowered trillium age gracefully to violet-pink.

little bluestem

Schizachyrium scoparium

dry upland prairies, sand savannas, roadsides

full sun

Little bluestem is most beautiful in fall, especially when the feathery white hairs of its ripe seed fruits are backlit by low light; many songbirds seek the seed fruits in that season. Some plants are noticeably bluish in the growing season; all turn rich reddish orange shades in autumn and hold this warm color well through winter without bleaching out. This upright clump-forming grass self-sows only lightly, so is suitable for traditional landscapes. It grows 30–40 inches tall and makes a fine mass planting or a component in a perennial border. It is integral to a prairie garden, especially in drier soils. Little bluestem grows best in full sun and just about any well-drained soil; some regional strains can be floppy in soils that are too rich.

Little bluestem is a great choice for a scrim.

The fall color and illuminated backlit awns of little bluestem make it one of the showiest prairie grasses.

maidenhair fern
Adiantum pedatum

moist upland forests

part to full shade

Maidenhair fern is always an ornamental standout in any setting. The fan-shaped leaf is doubly compound and finely sublime. The dark purplish black stalk splits into two, each half circling around with radiating stems of fin-shaped leaflets. This fern is a popular choice for traditional shade and woodland gardens and grows very well in containers, too. It is a prime candidate as a companion plant to spring ephemeral woodland wildflowers, holding their place (and your interest) in the garden after they go dormant. Give maidenhair fern moist, well-drained soil and at least afternoon shade. Can be divided to create still more plants.

Maidenhair fern is like no other and is possibly the most beloved of all native ferns.

marginal wood fern

Dryopteris marginalis

moist forests, woodlands

part to full shade

This and all wood ferns take readily to moist, well-drained soil in shady gardens, spreading slowly by rhizomes into multicrowned plants that can be divided. They make beautiful additions to traditional shade and woodland gardens, where they can be planted en masse or integrated with other spring ephemerals or woodland plants. Their doubly pinnately compound fronds add a very fine texture to the garden; they are more leathery than the fronds of other ferns, remaining evergreen but lying flat in the winter. Marginal wood fern is easy to identify because its spores line the margins of its leaflets (hence its names) and its fronds are more bluish green. It reaches a height of just 18 inches and is found in more acidic soils of sandstone or chert but grows well in most any well-drained woodland garden soil.

The distinctive marginal spores of marginal wood fern.

marsh blazingstar

Liatris spicata

moist to wet prairies and savannas

full sun to part shade

This is the most common blazingstar in cultivation. Dense flower heads give a wandlike appearance to the 3- to 5-foot flowering stem, and the lavender-purple (occasionally white) flowers are visited by butterflies and other pollinators. The tall, wand-flowering blazingstars are lovely in traditional perennial borders, pondside or wetland gardens, and in rain gardens. All produce whitened tufts of fruit that are quite attractive in the fall, but they quickly disintegrate and disperse the seeds. Plant this dazzling native wildflower with the similar prairie blazingstar, as marsh blazingstar will bloom first in midsummer, with prairie blazingstar following, extending the bloom season into late summer. They quickly make a spectacular display in rich, wet soils. This species does well in average garden soil; it thrives in wet locations in full sun or just a bit of shade. Its strain 'Kobold' is readily available at nurseries.

Marsh blazingstar in midsummer bloom on the Gensburg-Markham Prairie, Cook County, Illinois.

marsh-marigold
Caltha palustris

wetlands, wet prairies, sedge meadows

full sun to part shade

Marsh-marigold is a spring ephemeral, emerging quickly as soon as the ground thaws, blooming, setting seed, and often dying by midsummer. The early emergence of marsh-marigold's vivacious, molten yellow flowers make it the most dazzling spring wetland wildflower; plants often form mystical rivers or masses of gold in springs, seeps, and fens. In the right wetland habitat, it makes a remarkable spring-blooming perennial, growing to 2 feet tall. Plant it with cinnamon and royal ferns or tussock sedge to create a memorable composition in the garden. Marsh-marigold needs constant moisture to survive, even while dormant. Propagate by division.

The brilliant flowers of marsh-marigold burst from the meltwaters of spring.

marsh phlox

Phlox maculata

wet prairies, sedge meadows, floodplain forests

full sun to part shade

Marsh phlox's chief ornamental attribute is its strikingly vibrant fuchsia-pink (rarely white) flowers, borne in an elongated cluster. The early summer flowers are rich in nectar and visited by long-tongued insects, including butterflies and sphinx moths, as well as by hummingbirds. The stems too are spotted and streaked with purple, and the plant grows 2–3 feet tall, forming an upright clump suitable to a traditional perennial border where irrigation is available to keep the soil moist. Marsh phlox may be cultivated in moist organic or humus-rich soils, but it thrives in wet soils. It's an ideal plant for a rain garden, water garden, or wet prairie garden; include it at the bottom of a downspout or other landscape site that receives extra moisture.

Take a cue from its name, and give marsh phlox a damp spot if it is to thrive.

Marsh phlox has distinctive upright clusters of flowers.

Maximilian sunflower

Helianthus maximiliani

upland prairies

full sun

Maximilian sunflower is a conspicuously showy perennial, with early fall flowers of a rich, true yellow produced along much of the length of its tall flowering stem, not just at the top. The leaves too are very handsome: narrow and folded, arched downward, and an unusual gray-green. This less-aggressive sunflower does form a clump and is suitable for gardens, where it will grow well in any well-drained soil. It grows 5–6 feet tall in dry soil but will be taller in good garden soil. It is a perfect sunflower for a natural landscape or prairie garden, with the larger grasses as competition; however, it is a bit too seedy for traditional perennial borders.

Maximilian sunflower produces tall spires of classic yellow sunflowers.

meadow blazingstar

Liatris ligulistylis

moist upland prairies, roadsides

full sun

Meadow blazingstar has the lavender-purple flowers so typical of the prairie's floral color scheme, although the odd white-flowering form does occur. All blazingstars produce whitened tufts of fruit that are quite attractive in the fall. This button-type blazingstar blooms in late summer and fall, and along with rough blazingstar is among the best sources of nectar for fattening up the monarchs as they migrate. I've witnessed both species adorned with flocks of these butterflies, a sight I hope future generations will enjoy. The button-type blazingstars are best in a more natural landscape or planted in a mass among smaller prairie grasses, such as sideoats grama, little bluestem, and prairie dropseed. Meadow blazingstar is usually in peak bloom around Labor Day, its loose clusters of flowers along stems that grow more than 2 feet tall.

Migrating monarchs cannot resist the nectar from meadow blazingstar on a prairie remnant near Decorah, Iowa.

Midland shooting stars

Dodecatheon meadia

prairies, savannas, woodlands

part to full shade

This wildflower is beloved for its downward-pointed "beaklike" pistil and its exquisite corolla of upswept petals, which may be white to deep rose, and every hue in between. The basal leaves emerge in early spring. The flowers are produced atop 12- to 30-inch scapes; they are pollinated by queen bumblebees that buzz while hanging upside down from the flowers, thus releasing their pollen (there is no nectar). The fruiting capsule ripens brown and holds well into winter. Midland shooting stars makes a glamorous addition to any landscape, from a traditional perennial border to a natural garden. Plants thrive in humus-rich, well-drained soils that are moist in spring. They go dormant by midsummer, occasionally lingering much later in moist conditions, so are well adapted to summer droughts. Propagate by dividing the dormant plant.

The downward-pointed flowers of Midland shooting stars are designed for bumblebees.

Missouri black-eyed Susan
Rudbeckia missouriensis

rocky prairies, savannas, woodlands

full sun to part shade

This long-lived perennial blooms in late summer, offering an abundance of classic black-eyed-Susan-style inflorescences, with glowing orange-yellow ray flowers surrounding the dark brown cone of disc flowers. The seed heads hold well into winter on stems over the evergreen basal foliage. Missouri black-eyed Susan is a premier plant for a traditional full-sun perennial border, growing 24–30 inches tall. It's a fine nectar and pollen plant for any insectaries garden. This Ozark Highlands endemic grows well in moist garden soil. Clumps are easily divided. Hardy throughout the Midwest.

Missouri black-eyed Susan paired with royal catchfly—a stunning combo.

narrow-leaf purple coneflower

Echinacea angustifolia

dry upland prairies

full sun

Another great native, very similar to pale purple coneflower, for a traditional perennial border in full sun. It demands perfect drainage and tolerates extreme heat and drought. Don't deadhead: it may self-sow if you're lucky, and the birds will appreciate the seed heads, into winter, as much as the butterflies did the early summer blooms. Each light purple flower is held on a stout single stem. Flowers are rich in nectar and attract a wide range of pollinators, including a certain mining bee, *Andrena helianthiformis*, that utilizes only this and pale purple coneflower. The interesting seed heads are really something to look at and are especially pretty when adorned with snow.

Narrow-leaf purple coneflowers, awaiting mining bees.

Great spangled fritillaries vie for nectaring space atop narrow-leaf purple coneflower.

New England aster
Symphyotrichum novae-angliae

moist to wet prairies, moist sedge meadows, roadsides

full sun to part shade

New England aster is a regal sight from earliest fall to the first frosts of late autumn, when its purple flowers with yellow centers may be beautifully covered with migrating monarchs and other late-season butterflies in contrasting yellows and oranges. It and its cultivars are well-known perennials, growing 4–6 feet tall and, with that height, frequently used at the back of a traditional perennial border or as an informal hedge. New England aster prefers moisture and can lose its lower leaves and look scraggly if its situation is too dry. Plants are at their best in a wetland garden or rain garden, where they have extra moisture. They produce seedlings abundantly in some settings, which makes them a great choice for natural gardens. And they are, along with aromatic aster, premier plants for insectaries and butterfly gardens. Can be overly exuberant in rich garden soils without competition. If plants grow too tall and gangly, cut them back before late summer, and they will still bloom.

The royal purple flowers of New England aster contrast well with autumn grasses.

oak sedge

Carex albicans

moist woodlands

part to full shade

I have to admit, I gardened with various woodland sedges for a decade before I had them all identified to species. They look like tufts or masses of grass, but they have V-shaped (in cross section) leaves from triangular stems—or, as the botanical adage goes, "sedges have edges." Many sedges are quite similar, and their cultivation, garden use, and attributes are little studied, but I haven't met one I would call aggressive or otherwise unwelcome in the garden. In the wild, oak sedge grows in second-growth woods with oaks and eastern red cedars. In cultivation, it prefers good garden soil in light shade. Oak sedge grows about 12 inches tall and wide. Perfect for the shade garden or adding interest to the winter garden.

Oak sedge, seen here on the winter solstice, produces a mound of very fine green leaves that hold well through winter.

Ohio goldenrod

Solidago ohioensis

interdunal wetlands, wet prairies, sedge meadows

full sun

Ohio goldenrod is a Great Lakes endemic. Its yellow flowers, in flat-topped clusters in late summer and early fall, are among the largest of the goldenrods. The foliage is handsome: the upward-pointing stem leaves are lance-shaped but with a blunt upper end; the basal leaves are wider and make a showy tuft even without a flower stalk. Fall color is often a rich burgundy-red. Plants grow 3–4 feet tall and are best in rich, moist soil. This magnificent goldenrod is suitable for a water garden, wetland garden, or rain garden but can also be used in a traditional perennial border, as long as the soil is rich in clay or remains moist.

Ohio goldenrod glows in the early autumn sun at Illinois Beach State Park.

pale leather flower

Clematis versicolor

woodlands, woodland edges

part sun to part shade

Pale leather flower is more tolerant of dry conditions than you would guess from its native woodland habitat, as it often grows on rocky glades. Probably the most ornamental of the leather flowers, it always grabs attention while in full bloom in mid to late summer and while fruiting and blooming in late summer and fall. Flowers are rosy purple to rosy lavender, fading to creamy greenish on the recurved tips of the sepals for a nice two-toned look. The fruits are the showiest of the herbaceous clematis, displaying a luminous bouffant of silky-awned achenes. A great vine for traditional landscapes. Try it on a trellis at the back of a border or against a home or arbor.

The silky plumed fruit of pale leather flower captures light when backlit.

pale purple coneflower

Echinacea pallida

dry upland prairies

full sun

The early summer flowers of this refined perennial are sublime—drooping straplike ray flower "petals" in a soft, creamy pink, surrounding a spiny orange-brown cone of disc flowers, each dotted with white pollen on top. They attract a wide variety of pollinators. The flowers are set above foliage that is seldom over 12 inches tall; plants may reach 30–36 inches tall. The sharply spiny seed heads turn almost black in winter and hold well all the way until spring. Pale purple coneflower is a denizen of hill, gravel, or otherwise rocky prairies in nature, so give it lean, well-drained garden soils. It is suitable for the perennial border, where it does exceedingly well in droughty locales with poor soil. Plants have failed in traditional landscapes that are fertilized and irrigated. Hardy throughout the Midwest.

Pale purple coneflower stands tall in a prairie border at Powell Gardens, Missouri.

palm sedge

Carex muskingumensis

swamps, open floodplain forests, sedge meadows

full sun to part shade

The overall look of this perennial sedge is indeed reminiscent of a palm, with whorls of three arching leaves in interesting tufts all along the stem. And palm sedge has high wildlife value, producing copious seed fruits for water birds and songbirds. The arching fruiting heads are pretty in summer and turn golden brown when ripe. Plants grow about 3 feet tall. This native sedge is an excellent choice for a rain garden, retention basin, or wetland garden; it will thrive in rich, continually moist to wet soils in full sun to light shade.

Its unusual foliage makes palm sedge one of the easier sedges to identify.

Pitcher's leather flower

Clematis pitcheri

woodlands, woodland edges

part sun to part shade

The flowers of Pitcher's leather flower always look like an upside-down urn, but they vary in color from solid royal purple to steely blue-purple to bicolored blue-purple with creamier sepal ends. Although the flowers are not showy from afar, they are beautiful on close inspection, which hummingbirds are all too happy to give them. The fruits are less showy than those of other herbaceous clematis, with shorter silkless-awned achenes. This deciduous vine is the most vigorous of our leather flowers, growing as much as 10 feet in a season and then dying back to the ground each fall. Perfect for cottage gardens, mixed borders, or perennial beds. Can be planted on trellises at the back of a border or against a home or arbor, or allowed to ramble over or through larger perennials and shrubs without smothering them.

Pitcher's leather flower rambles companionably through perennial plantings.

plantain-leaved sedge

Carex plantaginea

moist forests

part to full shade

Like most woodland sedges, plantain-leaved sedge transplants with ease. It reaches a height of 6 inches with a spread of 15 inches and can be used in shade gardens, en masse, to edge beds, or between stepping stones. When I created paths in my woods, I moved and saved every woodland sedge. I also leave or move sedges that self-sow in woodland garden beds. Just be sure to notice the ultimate size of unidentified wild species before moving them. Sedges produce seeds that are consumed by many songbirds, and their foliage is host to moths and butterflies. Consider this and all sedges, then, as an environmentally sound replacement for lilyturfs and mondo/monkey grasses, which offer little to native insects and wildlife.

The comparatively wide, noticeably seersuckered leaves of plantain-leaved sedge are quite distinctive and evergreen.

prairie blazingstar

Liatris pycnostachya

moist to wet prairies, sedge meadows, fens

full sun

Prairie blazingstar is another native well suited to a traditional full-sun perennial border. In a garden, it performs well in humus-rich loamy soil, its dense flower heads giving a wandlike appearance to the 3- to 5-foot flowering stem. Blazingstars are one of the few perennials that bloom from the top of the stem sequentially to the bottom. They are amazingly rich in nectar and attract a wide array of pollinators, especially butterflies. Seed fruits make an excellent food source for birds and other wildlife. Let your blazingstars self-sow, or you may lose them.

Prairie blazingstar forms a sweep of purple in a perennial border at Powell Gardens, Missouri.

prairie dock

Silphium terebinthinaceum

moist to dry prairies, savannas, glades, fens

full sun to part shade

Prairie dock breaks the mold of prairie plant leaves, which are usually cut or divided to reduce heat gain in full sun. Instead, each prairie dock leaf has short, raspy hair tufts that hold a layer of air against its surface, which makes the leaves feel cool, even on a hot day. Leaves blacken and curl up in a freeze but remain interesting in the winter landscape, when ther tufts are noticeably whitened, giving plants a polka-dotted "guinea hen" look. Flower heads open from elegant round buds that produce bright yellow ray flowers. The naked flower stalks tower above the 24- to 30-inch-tall leaves, growing 5–8 feet tall. Prairie dock grows in almost any soil type, and its spectacular large leaves make it a great foliage plant for the garden. Flower stalks can be floppy in shady conditions. Self-sows readily, soon becoming a mass planting in traditional landscapes.

prairie dropseed

Sporobolus heterolepis

prairies, open ground, disturbed ground

full sun

This warm-season grass, the most widely cultivated of our native grasses, looks fine alone or in mass plantings. It grows in tidy clumps 18–24 inches tall consisting of outward-arching leaf blades. Flowering occurs in late summer and early fall; the airy inflorescences borne atop the foliage reach 30–40 inches tall and emit an aroma reminiscent of popcorn; they are especially sparkly when backlit. The plant turns golden in autumn and holds a yellowish tan color all through winter. Prairie dropseed is eminently suitable for a traditional landscape, planted en masse or as an addition to perennial borders. It grows in just about any well-drained soil. Plant plugs to ensure it establishes successfully. Propagate by dividing clumps. Almost never self-sows.

The large leaves of prairie dock provide a shadow box canvas to its lengthening flower stalk and developing flower buds.

The finely textured blades of prairie dropseed are ornamental year-round at the Missouri Botanical Garden.

prairie onion

Allium stellatum

upland prairies, rocky prairies, glades

full sun to part shade

This onion (aka fall glade onion) produces a showy pink "golf ball" of flowers from late summer to early fall, eventually forming lovely seed heads adorned with black fruits. Prairie onion grows about 2 feet tall from a bulb; it is tolerant of extremely hot and dry conditions, which makes it particularly suited to rock gardens and other challenging "hell strip" sites. It will grow just fine in traditional landscapes and perennial borders as well, as long as you give it the well-drained soils it requires. Self-sows almost aggressively.

Prairie onion becomes a spectacular ornamental onion when grown in a garden setting, as seen here at Powell Gardens, Missouri.

prairie smoke

Geum triflorum

moist to dry prairies, glades

full sun to part shade

It is a must to experience this perennial in fruit on a windswept prairie. Its pendent spring flowers are maroon-red in clusters of three—not particularly showy but worth watching as large bumblebees pollinate them. Each pollinated flower produces an exquisite fruit that looks like smoke over the prairie when in mass and observed from a distance. The fruiting plumes grow just 12 inches above the basal foliage, which is attractive, being deeply lobed and evergreen. Prairie smoke is suitable for a rock garden, raised perennial border, or challenging "hell strip," as it thrives in dry sites. It makes a fine companion to diminutive plants, but its basal foliage must not be overshaded by more robust perennials, or it will die out. In a prairie garden, it is best planted in the company of shorter grasses. Prairie smoke is found on alkaline soils in nature. It is hardy throughout our region but requires good drainage and air circulation in the Lower Midwest.

The fruits of prairie smoke give the plant its common name.

prairie trillium

Trillium recurvatum

forests, woodlands, savannas

part to full shade

Trilliums are beloved woodland wildflowers, with three leaves and three petals. This trillium grows about 12 inches tall and can be used for naturalizing in woodland gardens. The petals curve upward like a bud; the sepals fall downward. The leaves are beautifully mottled green with burgundy splotches. Despite its common name, prairie trillium does not grow on prairies. It is probably the easiest of our trilliums to grow in a garden and quickly multiplies into a clump of many flowering stems. Propagate by dividing its thick rhizome; this is best done as the plant goes dormant in late summer or fall.

Prairie trillium is a robust grower and quickly forms a colony of flowering stems.

purple coneflower

Echinacea purpurea

moist to dry upland savannas, woodlands, prairies

full sun to part shade

Purple coneflower is a popular perennial throughout our region, widely planted in prairie gardens and naturalizing almost everywhere. The showy rosy pink ray flowers surround an orangish cone of disc flowers, blooming from midsummer and sporadically into fall. The flowers are very rich in nectar, attracting many pollinators, including butterflies. It's a preferred host plant for the silvery checkerspot, whose young caterpillars feast in little armies, prettily skeletonizing some leaves. The fruiting heads are spiny, ripen almost black, and are quite showy in winter, especially when capped with snowfall. American goldfinches seek the seeds as soon as they are formed. Very popular in all styles of landscaping, purple coneflower is often massed in perennial borders. It may self-sow into dense plantings, and allowing it to do so is a good idea because it is fairly short-lived. It is stunning mixed with other wildflowers and grasses and is at its best in a semishady natural garden.

Purple coneflower flowers prolifically at Powell Gardens, Missouri.

purple giant hyssop

Agastache scrophulariifolia

moist to dry upland savannas, woodlands, woodland edges

full sun to part shade

Purple giant hyssop is quite similar to yellow giant hyssop, only with pale bluish or purplish florets. Its common name overstates the reality of its light-colored flowers, as the photo shows, but they are as rich in nectar as both anise hyssop and yellow giant hyssop and appreciated by an equal cloud of pollinators. Purple giant hyssop grows as large as yellow giant hyssop, 2–5 feet tall, and has similarly simple cultural requirements: just give it well-drained garden soil. Its showy fruiting heads look great at the back of a perennial border or in the winter landscape.

The tall sturdy flower stalks of purple giant hyssop provide great contrast to late summer's many yellow-flowering composites.

purple milkweed

Asclepias purpurascens

upland savannas, prairies

full sun to part shade

All milkweeds are premier insectaries plants that attract hordes of butterflies and other pollinators; they are the sole host plant for the monarch. Purple milkweed produces an abundance of showy flowers, in full-rounded umbels of rose-purple; these are followed by upright, cylindrical pods. This short-lived perennial is probably the milkweed most suitable to a traditional perennial border, as it has no underground rhizomes. Purple milkweed prefers part shade but will grow just fine in full sun too. It grows best in moist soils, including heavy clay.

Another slightly misleading common name: purple milkweed blooms are a royal shade of rose, not true purple.

queen-of-the-prairie

Filipendula rubra

wet prairies, open wetlands, seeps, fens

full sun to part shade

"Cotton candy on a stick" best describes the plant in midsummer, when frothy masses of pearly round buds open to carmine-pink blossoms with a darker center and stamens. The flowers produce reddish seed capsules that ripen to brown and persist into winter; the tall fruiting head is quite showy in the winter landscape. The foliage, mainly deeply lobed basal leaves, is also beautiful. Queen-of-the-prairie makes a fine back-of-the-border perennial in a traditional garden, where it reaches 4–5 feet in height. It makes a nice mass and spreads slowly into a clump, never running amok or self-sowing. It is a magnificent plant for rain garden, wetland garden, or pondside, growing well in moist, rich garden soil but at its best with extra moisture. Flowers robustly in full sun but will survive in part shade. Usually propagated by division. Virtually all plants in cultivation are the cultivar 'Venusta'.

Queen-of-the-prairie adds its glorious pink flowers to a Michigan prairie garden.

rattlesnake master

Eryngium yuccifolium

moist prairies, savannas

full sun to part shade

The sturdy, lightly forked stems of this very distinctive perennial are crowned with spiny white, 1½-inch domed flower clusters. The basal foliage is spiky and bluish green—reminiscent of a yucca. The mature stems hold well into winter with striking brown seed heads. Plants grow to about 4 feet tall and make a striking addition to a perennial border. Rattlesnake master makes great mass plantings and serves as an integral component in a prairie garden, where it holds its own in competition with other wildflowers and prairie grasses. It is an incredible insectaries plant, attracting many pollinators including small butterflies. Rattlesnake master grows well in good garden soil. Self-sows abundantly when cultivated without mulch or competing plants.

Rattlesnake master in bloom shares the stage with marsh blazingstar on the Gensburg-Markham Prairie, Cook County, Illinois.

Riddell's goldenrod

Solidago riddellii

wet prairies, sedge meadows, seeps, fens

full sun

The rich yellow flowers of this wetland perennial are borne in dense, flat-topped clusters that tower above the plant. The lance-shaped stem leaves curve outward and downward. In autumn, flowers produce clouds of tufted white fruits that are relished by birds, and the leaves turn to a handsome dark burgundy. Riddell's goldenrod grows 3 feet tall and is suitable for traditional perennial borders in wet conditions, water gardens, rain gardens, and wet prairie gardens. Plants prefer moist to wet alkaline soil; they will require substantial irrigation to thrive in upland gardens.

The pointed, arching leaves beneath flat planes of yellow flowers identify this as Riddell's goldenrod.

riverbank grape

Vitis riparia

woodlands, hedgerows

full sun to part shade

Riverbank grape is well named, as it can be inundated by floodwaters for periods but still thrives in well-drained garden soils. Foliage emerges pink in spring; grape leaves are host to a wealth of insects. The fleecy green flowers go unnoticed to the eye but are extremely fragrant, demanding your olfactory attention when they bloom in late spring. Female plants produce the edible fruit. The vine's papery strips of bark are a favorite nest-building material of birds, used to line their nests. Wild grapes are easily cultivated, tolerating a variety of soils from moist to dry, but need full sun to thrive. Can grow 35–50 feet and sometimes more, climbing by tendrils that can wrap around any small object or cling to rough bark or even brick. Vines can be trained to a trellis. Weed out seedlings from formal beds, and trim them from various shrubs and trees they would otherwise overtake. It's worth the effort. I cannot imagine the home garden and landscape without this native grape.

Besides being attractive to wildlife, the beautiful fruits of riverbank grape are delicious for the table and in preserves.

rock honeysuckle

Lonicera reticulata

rocky upland woods, woodland edges, savannas

full sun to part shade

Why this great plant is not better known is puzzling. Near the branch ends, the paired leaves are fused into what looks like a single 3-inch-round leaf that the stem appears to pierce; these perfoliate leaves can be exquisitely waxy-coated, silvered or bluish, reminiscent of eucalyptus. Each branch end is studded with creamy yellow flowers that age to orange in late spring, followed by orange-red berries in fall. The nectar-rich flowers are visited by many pollinators, from hummingbirds to various bees; birds relish the fruit; and the foliage hosts several unusual caterpillars, most notably the hornworm of the snowberry clearwing, a day-flying sphinx moth that mimics a bumblebee. Rock honeysuckle is an ideal vine to climb up a small trellis or garden sculpture. Planted without support, it can take on a haystacklike growth, making you think it is a shrub. Easy to grow, to 6 feet or more in cultivation, in any well-drained soil. Extremely drought tolerant.

The warm bright berries and cool glaucous foliage of rock honeysuckle are real standouts in early autumn.

rose mallow

Hibiscus lasiocarpos

swamps, pondsides, riverbanks, wet ditches

full sun

The very showy flowers, 5 inches or more across, are white to various shades of rose—but always with a red eye, from which the column of stamens, tipped with a five-parted pistil, protrudes. The ornamental seedpod fruits look like short okra (its relative), turning blackish brown in late fall, opening to show the round seeds, and holding well on the plant through winter. Best grown in natural landscapes and an ideal subject for the shores of rivers, lakes, ponds, or other wet locales. Plants grow about 5 feet tall and can be planted in containers or in water gardens. The flowers are very rich in nectar and pollen, so are excellent choices for insectaries gardens. In nature, rose mallow will grow in standing water. In cultivation, it does just fine in good garden soil but prefers wet conditions.

The velvety, pleated-looking petals of rose mallow are usually white.

rose turtlehead

Chelone obliqua

marshes, sedge meadows, seeps, fens

full sun to part shade

Rose turtlehead is the perfect native for a traditional perennial border in wet conditions, or at least one that stays moist. Like white turtlehead, it prefers wet soils but will grow in continually moist garden soil—it languishes in dry conditions. Plants usually grow around 3 feet tall in a garden setting. The showy flowering spikes bear rosy pink flowers that are shaped like the heads of turtles and protrude from the stem. Hummingbirds and large bumblebees that are able to open and enter the flowers are responsible for pollination. The seedpod fruits ripen brown and stand tall for winter interest. Propagate turtleheads by division.

The flowers of rose turtlehead are nearly identical to those of white turtlehead but flushed with lavender-rose.

rosinweed
Silphium integrifolium

moist to dry upland prairies, savannas

full sun to part shade

Like all silphiums, rosinweed produces bright yellow flower heads in late summer that look like a sunflower and attract wide diversity of pollinators. The typical silphium seed fruits that follow often hold like flower petals; they are oily and relished by songbirds. The foliage is also beautiful, the leaves paired along the stem like miniature cup plant leaves. Rosinweed makes a stout, 4- to 5-foot tall perennial for the back of a perennial border and is an important component of prairie gardens and other natural landscape plantings. It grows readily in average garden soil and does not self-sow as aggressively as cup plant or prairie dock.

The sunny yellow flowers of rosinweed crown the plant in late summer.

rough blazingstar
Liatris aspera

dry upland prairies

full sun

Rough blazingstar offers flowers in loose, buttonlike clusters along its 2-foot-plus stem, and these come pleasingly late in the growing season, in September and October, when many gardens can use a shot of color. It requires good drainage in a garden setting and is extremely drought tolerant. Blazingstars are amazingly rich in nectar and attract a wide array of pollinators, especially butterflies. Most blazingstars form an underground corm that is a favorite food of voles, and many species are short lived, including this one. Losing plants to critters and a short lifespan translates into this gardening reality: let your rough blazingstars self-sow, or you may lose them.

Nothing says autumn on the prairie like the buttonlike purple flowers of rough blazingstar.

round-lobed hepatica
Anemone americana

moist upland woods

part shade

Hepaticas, one of the first wildflowers to bloom each spring, are botanical gems native across the Northern Hemisphere. The variation in flower colors and leaf patterns these diminutive plants offer makes them beloved and increasingly popular perennials—hepaticas are on the verge of becoming mainstream in U.S. gardens and landscapes, seen everywhere from containers to woodland and rock gardens to perennial border edges. In the wild, round-lobed hepatica is usually found in more sandy, acidic soils; however, it is tolerant of a range of soil types and pH levels in cultivation. Its flowers are virtually identical to those of sharp-lobed hepatica. The leaves are similarly three-parted but with rounded lobes, and they retain a fuzzier look through the season, sometimes showing an imaginative array of burgundy and silver patterning that is unmatched by any evergreen woodland perennial.

The leaves of round-lobed hepatica may have lovely patterning, as shown by this silvered specimen at Indiana Dunes National Park.

royal catchfly

Silene regia

moist savannas, prairies

full sun to part shade

Royal catchfly plants are few-stemmed and lanky, with inconspicuous paired leaves—so, ornamentally speaking, it's all about the screaming-red, five-petaled flowers that are borne in loose clusters atop the plant. The plant is upright and sturdy, growing 3–5 feet tall. In the landscape, it looks best as a companion to other plants, where its late-summer flowers can simply wow you. It is pollinated by the ruby-throated hummingbird. Royal catchfly grows very well and is long-lived in a garden setting in moist, well-drained soil.

A royal catchfly in bloom; this stand-alone specimen reveals the tall open form of this native perennial.

royal fern

Osmunda regalis

wetlands

full sun to part shade

Royal fern is beautiful from start to finish, beginning each spring with its coppery to purplish fiddleheads, followed by rich green fronds of compound leaves that turn golden in fall. The fertile fronds topped with golden spores mature brown and persist into winter. Plants grow around 3 feet tall in moist soils, but mature plants in ideal conditions may be 5 feet tall. A mature plant is almost shrublike or palmlike, creating a hummocky base. This is a magnificent fern for a streamside garden or lining a pond, and it makes a gorgeous container plant as well. In nature, it inhabits organic sandy or acidic soils; in cultivation, it will be slow growing in neutral or alkaline conditions. Mature clumps may be divided.

The maturing brown fertile fronds of royal fern.

sharp-lobed hepatica

Anemone acutiloba

moist forests, woodlands

part to full shade

The early spring flowers of this woodland perennial are something to look forward to; young plants will produce only a few flowers, but a mature clump can be crowned with them. The three-parted leaves with pointed tips are liver-shaped (hence liverleaf, another common name). The leaves are evergreen but usually turn burgundy in winter. This is a premier plant for an open shady woodland garden or edge of a woodland perennial border. As it grows just 6 inches tall, it's best displayed on rock walls or outcrops and planted with diminutive companions like moss, sedges, and smaller ferns. It makes a prime container plant for shade. Cultivate sharp-lobed hepatica in moist, shaded sites in calcareous soils. Larger plants can be divided. Hardy throughout the Midwest, but give it a more sheltered site in the western part of our region.

Sharp-lobed hepatica flowers are usually white but can be true blue (as here) or pink.

Short's aster

Symphyotrichum shortii

moist woodlands

part shade

Short's aster is my favorite of the woodland asters with very showy, rather full heads of possibly the truest blue flowers. Just like the prairie asters, these plants bloom in late summer or fall and add welcome seasonal color to a shade or woodland garden. Both flowers and seeds are attractive to a wide variety of songbirds. Short's aster is one of the better natives for a traditional perennial border in light shade. It's easy to grow in good garden soils and looks best in billowing masses.

Short's aster may just be the showiest of the midwestern woodland asters.

showy coreopsis
Coreopsis grandiflora

rocky prairies

full sun

Showy coreopsis is very similar to lanceleaf coreopsis but, despite what its scientific name would suggest, it has smaller, less golden flowers. Both it and lanceleaf coreopsis are hybridized into many cultivars with extra ray flowers and a longer flowering period, albeit still centered in summer. I haven't observed pollinating insects visiting the double-flowered hybrids, but I have seen them seeking the disc flowers of both this and lanceleaf coreopsis, and the seeds, when formed, support many songbirds. Showy coreopsis is a wonderful plant for a traditional full-sun perennial border; it is not as persistent in a garden setting as lanceleaf coreopsis, but it does self-sow readily.

Showy coreopsis produces bright yellow "grand flowers" in midsummer.

showy goldenrod

Solidago speciosa

moist to dry upland prairies

full sun to part shade

This goldenrod is one of the last of our prairie wildflowers to bloom, and its conspicuously ornamental pyramidal domes of golden yellow flowers will just as readily light up your home landscape each autumn, when a shot of fresh color is most welcome. Plants grow around 3 feet tall in the garden and often have phenomenal fall color, as the whole plant may turn red or burgundy after blooming. Showy goldenrod is an important component of natural landscapes and prairie gardens and a key late-season nectar source for migrating butterflies. It grows well in almost any well-drained soil and stays in a clump, so is suitable for a traditional perennial border. Rarely self-sows.

Showy goldenrod produces distinctive pyramidal flower clusters.

showy penstemon

Penstemon cobaea

dry prairies, glades

full sun

Showy penstemon is similar to large-flowered penstemon but is overall fuzzier and its flowers are light lilac to white. Bloom season is early summer; plants are 2–3 feet tall. Bumblebees pollinate the flowers, and the seedpod fruits that follow hold well into winter, extending the season of ornamental interest. It is easier than large-flowered penstemon to grow in average garden soil, but it too must be considered a short-lived perennial. Showy penstemon prefers rocky, well-drained soils, so it is best cultivated in a rock garden, above a wall, or in a container garden. It is also suited to natural gardens, where it can self-sow and persist.

Showy penstemon has the largest and most colorful flowers of our Midwest penstemons.

Shreve's blueflag iris

Iris virginica var. *shrevei*

wet prairies, swamps, sedge meadows, fens

full sun to part shade

Its swordlike leaves are attractive from emergence to autumn, but Shreve's blueflag iris is most beloved for its sweetly fragrant, lavender-blue to violet-blue flowers, whose falls are splotched with yellow and striated with black nectar guides for its many pollinators. It blooms in early summer, and flowers produce interesting seedpod fruits that ripen dark brown in fall. This iris grows 2–3 feet tall and is a good choice for mass plantings to control erosion, as its spreads moderately from sturdy, well-anchored rhizomes, forming clumps. It's also a good choice for rain gardens and the margins of lakes and ponds. Tolerates dryness better than many wetland perennials, but still blooms best in moist to wet soils. Shreve's blueflag may be grown in a traditional perennial border, in moist, rich soil, as long as it is occasionally divided.

The brief flowering of Shreve's blueflag iris creates an indelible impression in early summer.

sideoats grama
Bouteloua curtipendula

dry upland prairies

full sun

Sideoats grama is named for its inflorescence, which consists of spikelets that line one side of the stem. A single clump of grass can produce a full crown of these inflorescences. It's most beautiful when in bloom: the anthers are red, making each spikelet look like a firecracker. The plant looks great in fall, as it turns straw-colored, and the foliage holds well into winter. Sideoats grama is a warm-season grass that performs well in gardens in well-drained soil. It is a shorter clump-forming grass, rarely reaching more than 30 inches tall. It makes a fine addition to a traditional garden, looking good as a single plant or planted en masse. In a prairie garden, it mixes well with little bluestem and prairie dropseed but can be smothered by big bluestem, Indiangrass, and switchgrass. Self-sows modestly.

Sideoats grama crowns a hillock at Harlem Hills Prairie, Winnebago County, Illinois.

smooth aster

Symphyotrichum laeve

moist to dry prairies, savannas, roadsides

full sun

Smooth aster's waxy, bluish green foliage is attractive all growing season, but the plant's peak of beauty comes in late summer and fall, with its profusion of flowers, which are light lavender-blue with yellow centers that turn reddish at maturity. Plants usually grow 2–3 feet tall and make a fitting addition to a traditional full-sun perennial border. Smooth aster is just as handsome in a natural landscape or prairie garden, mixed in among smaller prairie grasses, such as sideoats grama, little bluestem, and prairie dropseed.

Smooth aster blooms on the Chiwaukee Prairie, Kenosha County, Wisconsin.

smooth phlox

Phlox glaberrima

moist to wet prairies, marshland edges, floodplain forest openings

full sun to part shade

Smooth phlox is quite similar to marsh phlox but with acid fuchsia-pink flowers with a stunning blue overtone on flattish umbels. Its leaves are narrow and show a fine texture in lovely contrast to most other perennials, even while not in flower. The plant grows 18–30 inches tall and is suitable for any perennial border that remains moist to wet, where it will form a multistemmed clump without running roots. Butterflies, moths, and hummingbirds pollinate its midsummer flowers. In the garden, smooth phlox requires continually moist, organic or humus-rich soils. It's an ideal plant for a rain garden, water garden, or wet prairie garden; include it at the bottom of a downspout or other landscape site that receives extra moisture. Self-sows sparingly.

Smooth phlox in a home landscape, blooming at the bottom of a downspout, where it receives extra moisture.

sneezeweed
Helenium autumnale

wetlands, floodplains, sedge meadows

full sun to part shade

Sneezeweed is impressively tall, growing to around 4 feet, and its memorably bright flowers, which bloom from late summer into fall, attract a wealth of small pollinators. The yellow flower head is composed of a button of disc flowers surrounded by a whirling skirt of notched "petals," the yellow ray flowers. This plant is suitable for a traditional perennial border, rain garden, pondside, or streamside setting; it grows in moist garden soil but is at its best when sited in a spot that receives extra moisture—another candidate for the bottom of a downspout! The many cultivars, some of more compact stature, offer colors ranging from yellow to orange and burnt reds, and combinations thereof.

Sneezeweed flowers are simply beautiful; they don't make you sneeze.

soft rush
Juncus effusus

wet prairies, sedge meadows, disturbed wetlands

full sun to part shade

Soft rush's spikily upright to arching clumps of blue-green tubular leaves look spiffy, and the foliage remains ornamental from summer through fall and into winter. The plant grows at least 2 feet tall and provides a tidy, tufted structure in a wetland, rain garden, or water garden, looking almost formal when planted in masses. It also makes a great container plant. In the garden, soft rush may be grown in moist soils but is best in wet conditions. Clumps are easily divided.

Two clumps of soft rush stand out in this streamside garden.

Solomon's seal

Polygonatum biflorum

forests, woodlands, woodland edges, roadsides

part sun to full shade

I've been enamored by the subtle beauty of this often magnificent perennial since childhood. The late-spring flowers, nodding beneath and somewhat hidden by the foliage, are whitish green elongated bells; they are quite rich in nectar and visited by many bees and hummingbirds. In fall, the leaves turn golden yellow, and the arching stalk is adorned with pendent blue berries at each leaf axil. This asparagus relative should definitely be included in food forests, as its shoots and short, spreading rhizomes are edible. Its architectural clumps of foliage are also suitable for a traditional garden's shady perennial border, and it makes an important subject in a shady insectaries or bird garden. Ideally, give Solomon's seal rich soil in a woodland garden. Clumps are easily divided.

Solomon's seal is most beautiful with ripe fruits and autumn foliage.

spinulose wood fern

Dryopteris carthusiana

moist forests, woodlands

part to full shade

This is the easiest wood fern to cultivate in Midwest gardens. Its dense scaly stalks, about 12 inches in height, arise in a circle from its rootstalk. All wood ferns take to moist, well-drained soil in shady gardens, spreading slowly by rhizomes into multicrowned plants that can be divided. They make beautiful additions to traditional shade and woodland gardens, where they can be planted en masse or integrated with other spring ephemerals or woodland plants. Their doubly pinnately compound fronds add a very fine texture to the garden year-round; they are more leathery than the fronds of other ferns, remaining evergreen but lying flat in the winter.

Spinulose wood fern in the winter garden—which explains why florists rely upon this evergreen fern for use in cut arrangements.

spotted Joe-Pye weed

Eutrochium maculatum

wet prairies, sedge meadows, fens, moist disturbed ground

full sun to part shade

The domes of rosy pink flower clusters atop this plant are its crowning glory, and when the plant is in its late-summer bloom, they form an ideal landing pad for butterflies. The leaves too are notable, whorled in three-somes or foursomes along the purplish or purple-spotted stem, and in fall, the plant is attractively covered in deli-cate tufted fruits. Spotted Joe-Pye weed can be used in tra-ditional perennial borders, where it grows 4–5 feet tall. It is a solution to a problematic wet site, perfect for a pondside or rain garden, and a must for a butterfly or insectaries garden. Do not fail to include it in the night garden, as it's a magnet for nocturnal moths. Spotted Joe-Pye weed grows well in good garden soil but performs best with adequate moisture and wet conditions. Divide large plants to prop-agate them.

In late summer, spotted Joe-Pye weed produces dramatic domes of pink flower heads above beautiful whorls of highly textured leaves.

spring polemonium
Polemonium reptans

rich upland woods, moist forests

full sun to part shade

Spring polemonium has showy lavender-blue flowers and ornamental foliage composed of pinnately compound paired leaflets. The light green calyxes stay on the plant after its spring flowering, turning yellow as the capsule of seeds inside them ripens. This clumping perennial grows no more than 15 inches tall and integrates well into a shady perennial border or woodland garden. Give spring polemonium shaded well-drained soils that are moist in spring. Self-sows lightly. Hardy throughout the Midwest.

Spring polemonium's flowers are an iconic if ephemeral component of Midwest woodlands in that season.

stiff coreopsis

Coreopsis palmata

moist to dry prairies, savannas

full sun to part shade

The midsummer flowers of stiff coreopsis are bright yellow and up-facing above the leafy stems. The leaves are unusual, slim and three-parted, giving plantings a fine-textured effect in the landscape. Stiff coreopsis grows around 2 feet tall. It's integral to prairie gardens, where its nectar-rich flowers attract many pollinators, and its fall and winter seeds are utilized by songbirds. It is easy to cultivate in any well-drained garden soil and spreads—but not obnoxiously so—via rhizomes into a larger colony. Stiff coreopsis cannot compete with lush and larger-growing plants; give it shorter grasses (such as little bluestem, sideoats grama, prairie dropseed) and wildflowers (pale purple coneflower, butterfly milkweed, leadplant) as companion plants. Easily propagated by division.

Stiff coreopsis spreads into spectacular masses of yellow flowers on the Paint Brush Prairie, Pettis County, Missouri.

stiff goldenrod

Solidago rigida

moist to dry upland prairies, disturbed ground

full sun to part shade

Stiff goldenrod's up-facing flat inflorescences of yellow flowers are not only distinctive, they have a very high wildlife value, being very rich in nectar for all sorts of pollinators and producing copious amounts of seed that songbirds savor. The large, strappy, gray-green basal foliage is also quite handsome, turning shades of orange and red in the fall, and when the seed fruits mature, each with a white crownlike tuft that helps carry it in the wind, plants have a particularly ornamental, frothy, almost floral look. This goldenrod thrives in any well-drained soil. It makes a fine garden plant if grown in poor, dry soil with established plants but becomes too gangly and will self-sow into a nuisance in rich garden soil without competing plants. It is best in natural gardens and prairie gardens.

Migrating monarchs mob a wild stand of stiff goldenrod on a private prairie remnant in Iowa.

stout blue-eyed grass

Sisyrinchium angustifolium

prairies, savannas, roadsides, disturbed ground

full sun

Blue-eyed grass is in the same family as irises, with showy flowers adorning the upper parts of the bladelike stems for a similarly brief period in mid to late spring. The flowers, which open only in sunshine, are usually violet-blue, sometimes white, but always with a touch of yellow in the center; they attract numerous pollinators. Seeds are produced in tiny brown globe-shaped capsules; they are relished by songbirds. Plants grow no more than 12 inches tall and remain tidy grassy tufts even when not in flower, perfect edging to a traditional or informal flower border and naturals for a prairie garden, as they are present in nearly all our prairie remnants. Give stout blue-eyed grass plenty of light and any moist, well-drained garden soil, and it's off to the races. Naturalizes readily.

A floriferous mass of stout blue-eyed grass edges a walk at the Missouri Botanical Garden.

swamp milkweed

Asclepias incarnata

wet prairies, sedge meadows, swamps, marshes, fens

full sun to part shade

Swamp milkweed is a host plant to the monarch and a must for insectaries gardens, as it attracts abundant insect pollinators. The up-facing, flat clusters of pink-and-white flowers (occasionally pure white) bloom in late summer and early fall. The dried plant, with its pod fruit remnants, is quite attractive in the winter landscape. Swamp milkweed grows 3–4 feet tall. It is best cultivated in moist to wet organic soils, pond- or streamside, but it tolerates clay soils and moist, well-drained garden soils. More and more, it and other milkweeds are included in traditional perennial borders, in support of monarchs, but (as its name suggests) this one really shines in water gardens, rain gardens, and wetland gardens.

The fragrant bicolored flowers of swamp milkweed host a wealth of pollinators.

sweet black-eyed Susan

Rudbeckia subtomentosa

prairies, disturbed open ground

full sun to part shade

The very showy flowers of this sturdy perennial are in the classic black-eyed Susan format of orange-yellow ray flowers surrounding a brown cone of disc flowers. The seed heads hold well into winter, adding ornamental interest. Sweet black-eyed Susan grows in moist, well-drained soil and, with plants topping out at around 5 feet tall, it makes a superb back-of-the-border perennial in more informal landscapes. It is best suited, however, to a natural landscape or prairie garden, where other plants can compete with it. Self-sows readily.

Sweet black-eyed Susan creates a mass of gold at Powell Gardens, Missouri.

switchgrass

Panicum virgatum

moist to wet prairies, floodplains

full sun to part shade

Switchgrass, one of the tall grasses of the prairie, is now a popular garden perennial with many available cultivars, including those with bluer or burgundy foliage. This classic warm-season grass flowers in late summer with a very airy open panicle of florets. It looks wonderful through fall when it goes to seed and even looks fine into winter. The foliage usually turns amber-yellow to orange in the fall and retains a warm golden blond look in the winter landscape. Switchgrass stays in a clump, usually grows 4–5 feet tall (some strains reach 8 feet), and can be readily maintained in a traditional perennial border; in a garden, it is tolerant of all types of soils. It's also used in rain gardens and swale gardens that collect stormwater runoff, and it makes a good hedge or seasonal screen. Local strains are appropriate in prairie gardens. Established clumps are easily divided. Self-sows lightly.

tall coreopsis

Coreopsis tripteris

prairies, savannas

full sun to part shade

Tall coreopsis, a common component of tallgrass prairies, is aptly named, easily towering 5–8 feet in open clumps. It makes an architectural statement in the home landscape, its sturdy vertical stems rhythmically tiered with neat three-parted foliage. The up-facing yellow ray flowers surround a dark center of red-brown disc flowers in midsummer, and the blackened seed heads of fall hold through winter. The entire plant can turn shades of orange to burnt red in autumn. Tall coreopsis thrives in moist, rich, well-drained garden soil; in poorer, drier soil, it is less aggressive and shorter. It makes a fine open screen or back-of-the-border plant but is at its best in a natural landscape mixed with native grasses and other wildflowers; without competition, it can be fairly aggressive in rich soil and self-sow abundantly. Easy to divide from a clump.

The airy panicles of switchgrass make it a garden standout in fall and winter. Shown here is *Panicum virgatum* 'Cloud Nine'.

Tall coreopsis produces a flat-topped cluster of flowers atop tall, leafy stems.

trumpetvine

Campis radicans

floodplain forests

full to part sun

Trumpetvine can be spectacular—in the right place. The large flowers bloom over a long period in summer; they are usually orange to almost red, rarely yellow, and are especially glorious when backlit. Hummingbirds pollinate them by day and sphinx moths by night, producing woody capsules that split down the middle and add a bit of interest to the vine in winter. The foliage is host to the plebeian sphinx moth. Trumpetvine spreads and suckers by underground rhizomes and climbs by rootlets that form along its stems and trunk; do not plant it against your home, as it can ruin siding and will sprout up all around the foundation. Rather, provide it with a tree, pole, or post out in the yard, where hardscape or a lawnmower can keep the suckers at bay. It's adaptable to all soil types except those that are excessively dry. Requires sun and will be weak and not flower in dense shade. Hardy throughout our region but give it a sheltered site in colder parts of the Upper Midwest.

Trumpetvine resembles a small tropical tree when trained on a low garden post.

tussock sedge

Carex stricta

wet prairies, sedge meadows, swamps, marshes, fens

full sun to part shade

It is shocking how little known this grasslike plant is in traditional landscaping. Tussock sedge makes a beautiful tufted mound of arching fine-textured foliage that looks great through the entire growing season as well as when dormant. It blooms in late spring with little-noticed spikelets and stays in a perfect clump (the proverbial tussock), growing about 2 feet tall and wide. Tussock sedge produces seeds that are sought by many ducks and songbirds, and it is a host plant to several wetland-dependent butterflies, including several skippers and satyrs. It's a nice structural plant for the lowest part of a rain garden or retention basin as well as for a wetland garden. Requires moist to wet organic soils. Propagate by division.

Tussock sedge emerges and blooms early, creating a crown of golden inflorescences amid fresh upright growth.

upland white aster

Solidago ptarmicoides

dry upland prairies, savannas, glades

full sun

Upland white aster blooms in late summer, its daisylike flowers borne in an open, airy dome above the basal foliage. The white flowers are rich in nectar and great for pollinators; later, songbirds seek the seeds. In the wild, upland white aster is found in the company of smaller plants able to survive in harsh conditions. In the garden, it is suitable for a traditional perennial border, providing the soil is very well drained. This aster grows just 12 inches tall, making it perfect for the edge of a border where larger perennials are not allowed to crowd it out. It's also a great choice for sites with droughty or rocky soils subject to hot afternoon sun—try it atop rock walls or in rock gardens. It thrives in such dry settings.

The starry white flowers of upland white aster.

violet wood-sorrel

Oxalis violacea

upland prairies, savannas, woodlands

full sun to part shade

Forget the various tender nonnative oxalis found in summer bulb catalogs: violet wood-sorrel, our native "shamrock" oxalis is a lovely ephemeral spring wildflower for traditional landscapes, prairie gardens, and woodland gardens. Its pale pink to violet-pink flowers appear in mid to late spring above the beautiful three-parted foliage typical of all oxalis. The leaves are bronzy or purplish-tinged beneath, and some plants have delightful dark burgundy markings on their leaf surfaces, which makes them highly ornamental foliage plants. The fruits are edible but contain oxalic acid, the same compound that gives rhubarb its tartness, so consider yourself warned. Birds love them. Violet wood-sorrel thrives in well-drained soils and can be naturalized in lawns. Propagate by division, right as plants go summer-dormant.

The pale five-petaled flowers of violet wood-sorrel contrast with dark blue violets.

Virginia bluebells

Mertensia virginica

floodplain forests

part to full shade

The flowers of Virginia bluebells mature from pink buds yet are mainly shades of blue, from soft smoky blue to medium porcelain blue—no photograph can do them justice. Plants grow 1–2 feet tall and may be used in traditional landscapes like any bulb that has spectacular spring flowers and then goes dormant by early summer. They are an essential component of natural woodland and shade gardens and perfect naturalized in a lawn or included for seasonal color in a traditional perennial border. Virginia bluebells thrives in deep loamy soils; it languishes in poorly drained clays or poor dry soils. Propagate by dividing the fleshy rhizome after the plant goes dormant. Self-sows readily.

Sedges make fine companions for this clump of Virginia bluebells at the Chicago Botanic Garden.

Virginia creeper
Parthenocissus quinquefolia

woodlands, woodland edges

full sun to part shade

This magnificent cloak of green will grow almost anywhere, and the foliage consistently turns fiery red in early fall as the inedible blue-black fruits ripen. The early fall color may draw the attention of birds, who seek its ripe fruit as important fuel for migration, and as host to many moths, it is one of the best plants for providing food for nesting birds, too. The flowers are little noticed but very rich in nectar for pollinators, including bees and hummingbirds. This beautiful vine climbs by tendrils with adhesive disks. It's a fine choice for covering almost anything with a curtain of living plant where no trellis is possible, and it's at its best when it grows as in nature: up and into a shade tree. It can also be used as a groundcover on steep banks and in woodland settings. Virginia creeper is easy to cultivate in any well-drained garden soil. It grows huge over time, readily 20 feet to over 50 feet, limited only by the structure upon which it climbs.

Virginia creeper climbs the stone facade near the entryway of a home.

Virginia mountain-mint

Pycnanthemum virginianum

moist to wet prairies, sedge meadows, fens

full sun

Virginia mountain-mint is a marvelous native herb with a fresh minty aroma that can be made into a tea. It grows well in good garden soil and tolerates being wet better than our other mountain-mints, forming clumps that may be readily divided. Plants reach 24 inches tall. Virginia mountain-mint is a perfect plant for a traditional full-sun perennial border and a healthy, ecologically sound landscape. It and all mountain-mints are superior choices for an insectaries garden, providing nectar for more pollinators and beneficial insects than virtually any other group of plants.

Virginia mountain-mint has the flat-topped white flower clusters characteristic of all mountain-mints.

virgin's bower

Clematis virginiana

moist woodlands, woodland edges

full sun to part shade

Virgin's bower is a blanket of white flowers during its midsummer bloom, but the feathery autumn seed heads on female plants are its most striking ornamental attribute. This easy-to-cultivate and rambunctious woody vine grows 8–15 feet in a garden setting, climbing by winding its leaf petioles around supports; it will readily cover a large arbor. It should be sited where it can be controlled around the edges and is best grown in natural landscapes along the edge of woodlands or along hedgerows, where it creates marvelous wildlife habitat. Virgin's bower is tolerant of a wide range of well-drained soils from moist to dry. It is easily propagated by division and can root wherever the stems touch the ground, which makes it suitable as a groundcover on steep embankments. You may prune back to stem buds in early spring, but cutting this vine to the ground will sacrifice flowers. Self-sows readily. Hardy throughout the Midwest.

Virgin's bower, here in bloom, cloaks a large post at the Minnesota Landscape Arboretum.

western sunflower
Helianthus occidentalis

dry upland prairies, savannas

full sun

Western sunflower is one of those less-aggressive sunflowers you can wholeheartedly welcome to your garden. Its wide basal leaves are a beautiful rich green from spring through fall. Its 2-inch flowers, borne on thin stems that are nearly leafless, open earlier than most wild sunflowers, in late summer. Western sunflower is of short stature, for a sunflower, and even in a garden setting, its smaller size makes it easier to control and prevents it from smothering most plants. Its flowering stems rise no more than 3 feet above low foliage. This perennial is suitable for planting in a poor, dry site in scorching sun, from "hell strips" to rock gardens. In rich soils, it will be overwhelmed by other plants.

Western sunflower in bloom at Nachusa Grasslands, Illinois.

white turtlehead

Chelone glabra

marshes, sedge meadows, seeps, fens

full sun to part shade

The showy spikes of milky white flowers bloom in late summer and early fall, and the seedpod fruits ripen brown and stand tall for winter interest. Turtleheads do best on the edge of a pond or stream, or in a wetland garden. They spread slowly by rhizomes, forming clumps, so are suitable for traditional perennial borders that remain moist. Plants usually grow around 3 feet tall in a garden setting. White turtlehead is the sole host plant for the dazzling Baltimore checkerspot butterfly across most of the Upper Midwest, where it overwinters in leaf litter as a caterpillar. You may see the butterfly at the Minnesota Landscape Arboretum's gardens and wild wetlands in midsummer. White turtlehead thrives in continually moist garden soil—it languishes in dry conditions. Propagate by division.

White turtlehead flowers are reminiscent of their relative the snapdragon.

white wild indigo

Baptisia lactea

moist to dry upland prairies, savannas

full sun to part shade

The foliage of white wild indigo is the most blue-green of the wild indigos and contrasts nicely with other plants. The early summer flowers are milky white in tall spires, showing well above the foliage, and followed by a showy spire of pea pod fruits that ripen from green to black and remain on the plant as an ornamental spire through most of winter. The pea pod splits open at some point in winter, in such a way that the plant audibly rattles as the two parts clap together; the seeds gradually lose their moorings and fall out. White wild indigo grows 4–6 feet tall (tip of the flower stalk) and looks best at the back of a traditional perennial border. It's superb in combination with shorter prairie grasses and is an integral component of a prairie garden. White wild indigo does well in almost any well-drained soil.

The flowering stem of white wild indigo stands as elegantly as the finest ballerina.

whorled mountain-mint

Pycnanthemum verticillatum var. *pilosum*

prairies, dry upland woods

full sun to part shade

Whorled mountain-mints reach 3 feet tall in full sun (2 feet in part shade), but whatever their size, mountain-mints epitomize a healthy landscape: they are superior plants for insectaries gardens, providing nectar for more pollinators and beneficial insects than virtually any other group of plants. I have found them to be perfect plants for a traditional perennial border, though they are rarely utilized that way. Whorled mountain-mint has slightly larger flowers than our other mountain-mints, with larger purple speckles that may produce more nectar; pollinators seem to choose it over Virginia mountain-mint. The first time I ever spied a dazzling white M hairstreak butterfly in a garden was on a large clump of this native perennial.

Whorled mountain-mint produces the largest individual flowers of our region's mountain-mints.

wild bergamot

Monarda fistulosa

prairies, meadows, savannas, disturbed open ground

full sun to part shade

Wild bergamot is a native herb with aromatic foliage that can be brewed into a tea. Its lipped, light lavender-purple flowers are elegantly exquisite, arranged in a whorl around a rounded flower head. Plants bloom in late summer in the Upper Midwest, when the larger, second-brood swallowtails are at their peak flight and readily congregate on the flowers for nectar. The foliage is exceedingly fragrant when rubbed or crushed; it is host to the hermit sphinx moth, a very important pollinator in general and the main pollinator of the endangered western prairie fringed orchid. The seed heads hold well into winter, retaining their bergamot aroma. Wild bergamot is easy to grow in any good garden soil, lightly spreading into a clump and reaching about 4 feet tall. It's suitable for a perennial border and a must for a natural landscape or prairie garden, as it thrives in disturbed ground. Propagate by division.

Wild bergamot's nectar-rich flowers are among the best natives for attracting bees and butterflies, including eastern tigers and giant swallowtails.

wild blue violet

Viola sororia

woodlands

part to full shade

Wild blue violet makes springtime gardens come alive with its beloved flowers (usually royal blue, rarely white). The flowers are edible, making this native perennial a nice component in an edible landscape and food forest; they are also host to several fritillary butterflies, including the spectacular great spangled fritillary, whose nocturnal springtime caterpillars can actually help keep this sometimes aggressive plant in check. (Note: this caterpillar emerges from its egg in fall and overwinters in the leaf litter—so raking up leaves essentially destroys it.) Wild blue violet is easily cultivated in any humus-rich soil that is moist in spring; it is at its best mixed among other woodland wildflowers. Plants can smother other diminutive plants, even taking over grass in a shaded lawn, and may go summer-dormant in drought conditions. Self-sows readily.

The common form of wild blue violet has deep blue-violet flowers and stems covered in short woolly hairs.

wild geranium
Geranium maculatum

moist to dry upland woods, savannas

full sun to part shade

A mature clump of wild geranium will produce an abundance of flowers, as showy in the landscape as any springtime azalea and lasting just as long, even in light shade. The palmate leaves are handsome, and the bright flowers eventually develop into beaklike fruiting pods that curl open from the base to disperse the seeds. Plants grow 1–3 feet tall; they can go dormant in dry years, but otherwise some basal foliage will hold until fall. This is a classic garden perennial; along with eastern red columbine and woodland phlox, it is a dazzling flowering component of the woodland garden in mid to late spring, best utilized en masse on the edge of woodland. Wild geranium attracts many pollinators, especially bees; a certain mining bee, *Andrena distans*, is a specialist on this wildflower. Grows in almost any moist, well-drained garden soil. Easily propagated by dividing mature clumps. Self-sows readily.

The vivacious violet-pink flowers of wild geranium are striated with nectar guides for pollinating insects.

wild hyacinth
Camassia scilloides

moist prairies, savannas, woodlands

full sun to part shade

The bladelike foliage of wild hyacinth emerges first, in early spring, followed by an airy spike of lovely bluish white to soft lavender-blue flowers. The flower spike grows 15–30 inches tall; fruits quickly mature and disintegrate. This beautiful perennial is on everyone's short list of specialty native bulbs for traditional landscapes; it makes a wonderful addition to both prairie and woodland gardens and should be included in food forests for its edible bulbs. Wild hyacinth thrives in humus-rich soil. It is slow to reach flowering size but worth the wait, and once established, a colony does multiply over time.

The midspring flowers of wild hyacinth are usually pale lavender-blue with contrasting yellow stamens.

woodland phlox

Phlox divaricata

floodplain forests, moist woodlands

part to full shade

The flowers of woodland phlox come in range of colors, from white to soft blue to rosy purplish; they are mainly pollinated by smaller sphinx moths, including the day-flying Nessus sphinx, snowberry clearwing, and hummingbird clearwing, and the dusk-flying lettered sphinx. Flower stalks are rarely more than 18 inches tall and quickly disintegrate. The evergreen foliage is mainly ground-hugging but sometimes disappears after spring, so this native does not make a good stand-alone groundcover. It does, however, combine well with almost any woodland plant, so may be integrated with shade-loving groundcovers or around larger shade perennials that maintain their presence through the growing season. Rabbits love this plant; give new plantings protection until established. Plant woodland phlox in any well-drained woodland soil in at least a partially shaded site. Very tolerant of summer drought. Self-sows readily in between established plants (but is never smothering) and even into a shady lawn; let it do so, or you may lose it. Hardy throughout the Midwest.

When woodland phlox is in bloom from mid to late spring, the magic of its flowers' delicate perfume fills the air.

wood poppy

Stylophorum diphyllum

moist forests over limestone

part to full shade

Wood poppy is a very adaptable and lush native perennial for a moist shade garden. The four-petaled golden yellow flowers, up to 3-inches across, are very showy. Each one is short-lived, but they bloom in sequence, mainly in spring, and smaller flowers can be produced into summer if rainfall is consistent. The foliage is heavily lobed and attractive. Plants grow around 2 feet tall but can go dormant during summer dry spells. Self-sows readily, overtaking less aggressive woodland garden plants. Hardy throughout the Midwest.

woolly pipevine

Aristolochia tomentosa

low woodlands, streamsides

full sun to part shade

My love for butterflies led me to include this twining vine: it is one of only two Midwest native plants that host the beautifully spectacular pipevine swallowtail. If you plant it, they will come: the butterflies lay their eggs on the foliage, and the caterpillars, once hatched, devour new growth, keeping the plant's growth in check. Woolly pipevine is aptly named: its large, heart-shaped leaves have a coating of hairs that make it very tolerant of heat and drought. The summertime flowers are quite a conversation piece. Plant two different-sourced plants to improve pollination, and you'll soon enjoy the simply beautiful podlike fruit that matures in autumn and dries out into 12-sided black capsules full of flaky seeds. Be sure to site this woody vine where you can embrace its large size and suckering root sprouts. It makes a phenomenal screening plant, covering many a large porch, but is nearly impossible to remove once established. Easy to grow in any woodland or organic soil, and easy to propagate from root divisions. Hardy throughout the Midwest.

Wood poppy's bright yellow flowers contrast perfectly with Virginia bluebells.

The bizarre flower of woolly pipevine.

wreath goldenrod

Solidago caesia

upland forests, woodlands

full sun to part shade

Goldenrods are essential components of a healthy woodland garden. In late summer and early fall, clusters of golden flowers adorn the leafy stems like a wreath, and this late bloom season, together with that of woodland asters, provides nectar for a host of pollinators and seed for songbirds. Wreath goldenrod reaches around 2 feet tall and makes a lovely mass planting; it also makes a fine companion plant, integrated with other woodland goldenrods, asters, grasses, and fall berries. In nature, plants usually occur in more acidic soils.

A blooming wand of wreath goldenrod reaches for the light along a woodland path at Indiana Dunes National Park.

Where happy, wreath goldenrod forms healthy stands.

yellow giant hyssop
Agastache nepetoides

moist to dry upland savannas, woodlands, woodland edges

full sun to part shade

We rarely design a landscape with the late-season hole created by dormant perennials in mind, but that's when yellow giant hyssop is at its showiest, bringing interest to the garden. The late-summer flowers are inconspicuous but very rich in nectar, with hummingbirds and other pollinators vying for position. When in bloom, the plant dances with swallowtails and hummingbirds and, later, goldfinches vie for position on its seed heads. The fruiting heads are marvelous atop exuberantly tall, sturdy stems, like torches in winter. Yellow giant hyssop grows 5–7 feet tall in well-drained moist soils in full sun to light shade. Plant it at the back of a perennial border with a woodland backdrop. It's best in a natural landscape, insectaries garden, or bird garden, as it brings in creatures, including deer (unusual for a mint), exceedingly well. Individual plants are short-lived but self-sow readily.

Yellow giant hyssop flowers show best where they will be backlit in the garden.

yellow purple coneflower

Echinacea paradoxa

prairies, glades

full sun

Both its scientific and common names aptly describe this paradox in the coneflower clan: its yellow floral pigments are what's behind the outbreak of beyond-purple coneflower hybrids. The leaves may grow about 12 inches high with flowers atop nearly bare stems reaching to 3 feet. The large flower head consists of bright yellow, 3-inch ray flowers that droop like a skirt around a 2-inch cone of rich reddish brown disc flowers. The dark, almost black fruiting head holds well into winter. Yellow purple coneflower doesn't run; it is well behaved and suitable as a traditional landscape perennial. In nature, this Ozark Highlands endemic grows in thin soil over bedrock. It demands good drainage and does best in full sun and scorching heat. Does not self-sow. Hardy throughout the Midwest.

Yellow purple coneflower grows abundantly with pale purple coneflower on the Paint Brush Prairie, Pettis County, Missouri.

zigzag iris

Iris brevicaulis

moist to wet forested slopes, ravines, floodplain terraces

full sun to part shade

Our native zigzag iris has been crossed with several other Louisiana irises to create a marvelous array of cultivars. It blooms in late spring after most woodland wildflowers are finished blooming, and the flowers are magnificent—4 inches across and royal blue, with yellow flares on the falls. This iris is relatively low-growing, reaching only 18 inches tall, and goes dormant through midsummer, reappearing in fall. In cultivation, it grows well in moist to wet garden soils in full sun to light shade, yet is very tolerant of drought. Best in a mixed perennial border, woodland garden, or rain garden. The spiky, swordlike foliage contrasts well with other spring woodland plants. Easy to divide. Hardy throughout the Midwest.

Unusually for an iris, both the falls and the standards of zigzag iris are upright.

Hardiness and Heat Zone Charts

USDA Plant Hardiness Zones

TEMP °F	ZONE	TEMP °C
−60 to −55	**1a**	−51 to −48
−55 to −50	**1b**	−48 to −46
−50 to −45	**2a**	−46 to −43
−45 to −40	**2b**	−43 to −40
−40 to −35	**3a**	−40 to −37
−35 to −30	**3b**	−37 to −34
−30 to −25	**4a**	−34 to −32
−25 to −20	**4b**	−32 to −29
−20 to −15	**5a**	−29 to −26
−15 to −10	**5b**	−26 to −23
−10 to −5	**6a**	−23 to −21
−5 to 0	**6b**	−21 to −18
0 to 5	**7a**	−18 to −15
5 to 10	**7b**	−15 to −12
10 to 15	**8a**	−12 to −9
15 to 20	**8b**	−9 to −7
20 to 25	**9a**	−7 to −4
25 to 30	**9b**	−4 to −1
30 to 35	**10a**	−1 to 2
35 to 40	**10b**	2 to 4
40 to 45	**11a**	4 to 7
45 to 50	**11b**	7 to 10
50 to 55	**12a**	10 to 13
55 to 60	**12b**	13 to 16
60 to 65	**13a**	16 to 18
65 to 70	**13b**	18 to 21

AHS Plant Heat Zones

ZONE	NUMBER OF DAYS PER YEAR ABOVE 86°F (30°C)
1	<1
2	1–7
3	>7–14
4	>14–30
5	>30–45
6	>45-60
7	>60–90
8	>90–120
9	>120–150
10	>150–180
11	>180–210
12	>210

Useful Resources

Armitage, A. M. 2006. *Armitage's Native Plants for North American Gardens*. Portland, Oregon: Timber Press.

Cochrane, T. S., K. Elliot, and C. S. Lipke. 2008. *Prairie Plants of the University of Wisconsin-Madison Arboretum*. Madison: University of Wisconsin Press.

Cullina, W. 2002. *Native Trees, Shrubs, and Vines*. New York: Houghton Mifflin.

——. 2008. *Native Ferns, Moss, and Grasses*. New York: Houghton Mifflin.

——. 2009. *Understanding Perennials*. New York: Houghton Mifflin.

Diblik, R. 2014. *The Know Maintenance Perennial Garden*. Portland, Oregon: Timber Press.

Diekelmann, J., and R. M. Schuster. 2002. *Natural Landscaping*. 2nd ed. Madison: University of Wisconsin Press.

Grese, R. E., ed. 2011. *The Native Landscape Reader*. Amherst: University of Massachusetts Press.

Grissell, E. 2001. *Insects and Gardens*. Portland, Oregon: Timber Press.

Harstad, C. 1999. *Go Native! Gardening with Native Plants and Wildflowers in the Lower Midwest*. Bloomington: Indiana University Press.

Hightshoe, G. L. 1988. *Native Trees, Shrubs, and Vines for Urban and Rural America: A Planting Design Manual for Environmental Designers*. New York: Van Nostrand Reinhold.

Hill, P. 2007. *Design Your Natural Midwest Garden*. Madison, Wisconsin: Trails Books.

Kingsbury, N. 2006. *Natural Garden Style*. London: Merrell Publishers.

——. 2014. *Gardening with Perennials: Lessons from Chicago's Lurie Garden*. Chicago: University of Chicago Press.

Moyle, J. B., and E. W. Moyle. 2001. *Northland Wildflowers*. Minneapolis: University of Minnesota Press.

Nowak, M. 2007. *Birdscaping in the Midwest: A Guide to Gardening with Native Plants to Attract Birds*. Blue Mounds, Wisconsin: Itchy Cat Press.

Oudolf, P., and H. Gerritsen. 2000. *Dream Plants for the Natural Garden*. Portland, Oregon: Timber Press.

——. 2003. *Planting the Natural Garden*. Portland, Oregon: Timber Press.

Oudolf, P., and N. Kingsbury. 2005. *Planting Design*. Portland, Oregon: Timber Press.

Porter, F. W. 2013. *Back to Eden*. Wilmington, Ohio: Orange Frazer Press.

Sawyers, C. E. 2007. *The Authentic Garden*. Portland, Oregon: Timber Press.

Simo, M. L. 2003. *Forest and Garden*. Charlottesville: University of Virginia Press.

Snyder, L. C. 2000. *Trees and Shrubs for Northern Gardens*. Chanhassen, Minnesota: Andersen Horticultural Library.

Steiner, L. M. 2010. *Prairie-Style Gardens: Capturing the Essence of the American Prairie Wherever You Live*. Portland, Oregon: Timber Press.

Sternberg, G. 2004. *Native Trees for North American Landscapes*. Portland, Oregon: Timber Press.

Tallamy, D. W. 2007. *Bringing Nature Home*. Portland, Oregon: Timber Press.

Tishler, W. H., ed. 2012. *Jens Jensen: Writings Inspired by Nature*. Madison: Wisconsin Historical Society Press.

Tylka, D. 2002. *Native Landscaping for Wildlife and People*. Jefferson City: Missouri Department of Conservation.

Van Sweden, J. 2011. *The Artful Garden*. New York: Random House.

Wasowski, S. 2002. *Gardening with Prairie Plants*. Minneapolis: University of Minnesota Press.

Weeks, S. S., H. P. Weeks Jr., and G. R. Parker. 2005. *Native Trees of the Midwest*. West Lafayette, Indiana: Purdue University Press.

Weeks, S. S., and H. P. Weeks Jr. 2012. *Shrubs and Woody Vines of Indiana and the Midwest*. West Lafayette, Indiana: Purdue University Press.

Acknowledgments

I would like to thank colleague Scott Woodbury, manager of the Whitmire Wildflower Garden at Shaw Nature Reserve, for all his work promoting native plants in the landscape.

I thank Mark Loeschke of the Iowa Department of Natural Resources for reviewing botanical accuracy and keeping me informed about all the new flora (and fauna) discoveries throughout the Midwest.

I thank Robert W. Dyas, professor emeritus at Iowa State University, for being my mentor and leading me and so many other landscape architecture students to natural areas in Iowa, Missouri, and Wisconsin, and to Iowa State University Professor Gary Hightshoe for all his inspiration, work with, and publications about native plants.

To Verne and Ardith Koenig, who took me on my first Audubon Christmas Bird Count in 1969; and to Bud Bahr, who was often in the birding party and shared so much of his botanical knowledge with me at such an early age.

To Neil Dieboll, Mervin Wallace, and Alan Wade for starting native plant nurseries well before they were cool and whose respective nurseries—Prairie Nursery, Missouri Wildflowers Nursery, and Prairie Moon Nursery—continue to supply Midwestern native plants and share how and why to grow them to gardener and restorationists alike.

To the Iowa Natural Heritage Foundation for saving some of my favorite sacred wild places along the Upper Iowa River and throughout Iowa.

To the Natural Land Institute for saving critical natural areas across north central and northwestern Illinois and for sharing their facilities for so many past programs and events. I will never forget their founder, the late George Fell, for his humble and unwavering pursuit of preserving natural lands and inspiring creation of Illinois Nature Preserves.

To the Missouri Prairie Foundation for protecting so much native prairie in Missouri and for carrying on the Grow Native! program that inspires the use of native plants across the Lower Midwest.

To all the other midwestern departments of conservation, departments of natural resources, parks departments, forest preserves, nongovernmental organization land trusts, and the Nature Conservancy, for all their work protecting the original homes of our native plants.

To the American Public Gardens Association and all their midwestern member gardens for conserving and displaying native plants, and educating visitors about their importance.

Lastly and most importantly I thank my parents and family for always embracing my pursuits and always being there to celebrate life's journey.

Photo Credits

Prairie Moon Nursery, page 6.

Shutterstock, pages 16, Ricardo Reitmeyer; 137, Dan4Earth; 146 (right), Peter Turner Photography; 178 (right), Jackie Robinson JR.

Marcie O'Connor, Prairie Haven, page 20 (top).

David Stonner, courtesy of the Missouri Department of Conservation, page 20 (bottom).

Kelly D. Norris, pages 40, 43, 44, 46, and 49.

Michael A. Dirr, pages 60 (left), 64 (left), 65, 66 (left), 69, 70 (left), 71 (left), 72, 74, 75 (left), 77 (right), 78, 79, 82, 93, 98, and 103 (left).

Flickr, pages 119, Doug McGrady; 132 (left), Michael Huft; 236 (right), Kristine Paulus.

Wikimedia Commons, pages 123 (left), 125 (right), and 147 (left), Krzysztof Ziarnek, Kenraiz.

Alamy, pages 170 (left), Gerry Bishop; 174 (right), REDA &CO srl, Paroli Galperti.

All other photos are by the author.

Index

About the Author

Connie L. Harclerode

Alan Branhagen is director of operations at the Minnesota Landscape Arboretum and the former director of horticulture at Powell Gardens, Kansas City's botanical garden. He is the author of *Native Plants of the Midwest* and *The Gardener's Butterfly Book* and has written articles for a range of publications, including *Fine Gardening*, *Missouri Gardener*, *Missouri Prairie Journal*, *Landscape Maintenance*, and *Restoration and Management Notes*. Alan is a naturalist and plantsman with a background in garden design and management; he specializes in botany, butterflies, and birds.

Copyright © 2020 by Alan Branhagen. All rights reserved.
Photo credits appear on page 244.

Published in 2020 by Timber Press, Inc.
The Haseltine Building
133 S.W. Second Avenue, Suite 450
Portland, Oregon 97204-3527
timberpress.com

Printed in China
Second printing 2021
Jacket design by Amy Sly
Text design by Debbie Berne

ISBN 978-1-60469-992-0

Catalog records for this book are available from
the Library of Congress and the British Library.

FSC
www.fsc.org

MIX
Paper from
responsible sources
FSC® C014688